MANAGEMENT USES

OF THE COMPUTER

MANAGEMENT USES
OF THE COMPUTER

by

Irving I. Solomon

Laurence O. Weingart

with Jerome Gartner, *Contributor*

HARPER & ROW, PUBLISHERS

NEW YORK AND LONDON

CONTENTS

ILLUSTRATIONS

PREFACE

This book is addressed to business people in middle and top management positions who must evaluate what computers can do for their companies. It is the outgrowth of some thirty man-years of experience (acquired unequally by the coauthors) with computers and their business applications; experience further refined through some ten man-years of teaching its conclusions to audiences much like the one envisioned for this book. We were agreeably surprised at the extent of our consensus on the principles set forth herein, in view of our disparate backgrounds. These principles, although not novel, deserve greater management attention before a specific company commits itself to the use of a computer in its business.

A nontechnical book on a technical subject must tread the narrow path between an overly complex treatment that will confuse many of its readers and an overly simple treatment that will not cover the subject properly. Trial presentations of this material have won the desired response from both business and technical audiences.

The book falls into four major divisions. The first of these examines the computer in the context of business data processing, offering perspectives on profitable computer usage in this application area, along with broad descriptions of computer capabilities. The intent is not so much to "sell" computers as to avoid selling them short. This section also presents some of the related technology and terminology needed to understand the material in subsequent sections of the book. This first section concludes with a capsule treatment of the remaining three sections.

The second section of the book considers the feasibility study, an examination of current business practices and information processing in the area being considered for conversion to computer processing. Although the feasibility study may seem to be unrelated to "automation" or to the application of computers to business data processing, it lays the necessary foundation for profitable computer application.

The third section of the book examines the continuation from a successful feasibility study to the development of a usable computer system and the selection of the proper computer to implement that system. For completeness, this section explores the alternatives to computer procurement for the application under study, and includes a discussion of the legal implications of computer usage (contributed by Jerome Gartner, LL.B.).

The final section of the book treats the problems of converting to the computer system and the continuing responsibility of management to maintain its usefulness. Here, as throughout the book, emphasis is placed on a systematic treatment of problems encountered and on treatment of the computer application as a system; i.e., a unified functional entity.

This book may not succeed in converting management personnel into systems analysts, but it travels that road to the point of diminishing return. A company president, or one of his immediate aides, facing the question of adoption of a computer can best answer it by becoming his own systems analyst. If the application is small enough, its analysis can be performed by following the guidelines given in this book; a by-product of this "do-it-yourself" approach will be the training to make best use of the resulting system. If the application is too large (or management is too busy) for a part-time analysis, this book affords management knowledge of the procedures and goals of systems analysis to assure more effective use of the outside analyst brought in for its performance.

Thanks are due to many individuals who contributed to this book without assuming any culpability for its failings. Dr. Denis Sinclair Philipps, Director of New York University's Management

Institute, earns this gratitude for his continuing support of presentations to management of the material embodied in this book. The American Management Association, in the persons of John K. Moore and John S. Dillon, afforded us the opportunity to expose our ideas to representative audiences. Our employers (Ernst and Ernst, and Computer Usage Company, Inc., respectively) deserve our thanks for their forbearance and encouragement while this book grew to completion. Finally, but not least in importance, we thank John Macrae whose editorial guidance led us to write this book rather than a different and poorer one.

Irving I. Solomon
Laurence O. Weingart

New York City
June 1966

PART 1

THE COMPUTER IN
BUSINESS DATA PROCESSING

The computer has been in business data processing since the spring of 1951 when the first commercially available business computer was installed at the U.S. Bureau of the Census. (This computer was retired, in 1964, to the Smithsonian Institution.) Within three years, duplicates of this computer were in use by a few large companies, a restriction explained by the monthly rental cost of around $25,000. By 1960, the computer industry was offering a range of smaller, faster computers at monthly rentals around $2,500, and since then the $1,000 per month barrier has been breached. This continuing trend toward smaller, cheaper computers and the wider availability of "part-time" computers for business applications is raising for more and more companies the question, "What can a computer do for me?"

The usual answer to that question is, "all your clerical work," yet the cost is seldom mentioned in the same breath. Although pioneer users of business computers dreamed of clerical cost savings to pay the cost of their computers, they found that the payoff came (if at all) from other, often not anticipated, sources. One group of computer users has profited from the astonishing speed of the computer. This group includes subscription list users (magazines, etc.) and mail-order companies. Subscription list users have found that computer speed allows them to update their mailing lists through the day preceding a mailing date, thereby reducing the number of misaddressed mailing pieces on which they pay return postage. In most cases, this saving alone covers the computer costs, making the gains from finer list breakdowns for selective mailings (also made possible by the computer) appear as pure profit. Mail-order firms have taken up the computer because its speed allows them to expand their product line without delaying their response to customer orders, and often without significantly increasing their investment in inventory. Their payoff comes from larger orders from more customers and from better return on their investment, apart from any savings on clerical costs.

In less specialized computer applications to business data processing, successful users have profited as much or more from reorganization of their data processing operations to meet business objectives more precisely as they have from reduced clerical costs. They get more, better, and faster data processing at about the same cost as for manual operations, which do less and do it less well. These computer users have thought through the implications of computer speed for their company's operation, departing from traditional methods when these departures offered better results. Computer designers say that their product is a "logical" machine. If successful business firms have profited from its use, it is more because they applied that kind of logic to their business operations, rather than it is the use of the logical machine itself.

WHAT IS
BUSINESS DATA PROCESSING?

Business data processing includes all flow of information needed to run a business. Traditionally, this information flow is divided into many separate elements, including:

1. Accounts receivable
2. Payroll processing
3. Accounts payable
4. Inventory control
5. Production scheduling
6. Production monitoring
7. Cost analysis
8. General ledger accounting
9. Any or all other elements of your choosing

The preceding list could be prolonged and modified indefinitely to match each company in any random assortment. As it stands, however, each element in it has something in common with all other elements, and therefore it is, or should be, one of the tools for efficient management of a business. Unfortunately, before the introduction of the computer (and other earlier devices for faster processing), these tools produced results of only historical interest because they indicated what should have been done in response to a particular situation, but gave this information one, two, or six months too late. Clearly, the speed of the computer can cut this lag from months to days or even hours, thus providing timely information on which to base management decisions. But, as we shall see, modification of existing systems is necessary, for the transfer of manual data processing operations, unchanged, onto a computer may produce unsatisfactory and even unprofitable results.

Manual data processing developed naturally as a piecemeal operation, gradually decentralized to handle immediate needs of the business it served. Its reporting periods differed for different elements in response to the needs and priorities of these elements. For example, payroll processing matches the payroll schedule (weekly, biweekly, or semimonthly in most cases), whereas production cost analysis may be reported only semiannually or annually, even though the production cycle is much shorter. If this decentralized, piecemeal approach is applied to computerized data processing, most of the advantages of the computer will be wasted. Getting a cost analysis on a six-week production cycle within a week after the close of the semiannual reporting period is a less significant improvement than getting the same report within a week after every production cycle. Furthermore, weekly payroll processing without coordinating weekly labor cost trend figures wastes the key advantage of computerizing business data processing. The computer is in itself a centralizing factor, pulling hitherto separate processing operations together to produce better-digested (i.e., more concise, while being more inclusive) information for management use, generally on a shorter reporting period. Judicious redesign of these reports is necessary, for when the computer is used to produce the same reports more often and more rapidly, management is drowned in an ocean of papers too large to be used. Pure speed is a mixed blessing in this case.

Computer users who have profited from their installations have done so because they adopted the *system approach* to their application. The system approach, pioneered by this nation's aerospace industry, calls for a survey of the forest before the trees are examined in any detail. Look back for a moment at the list of elements in business data processing; think of these elements as the trees, and consider instead the whole forest—the complete flow of information needed to run your business efficiently. If you think of this whole package as a system (i.e., something that can be isolated, with a definable functional goal, and thus susceptible to analysis without extensive consideration of external factors), you are likely to see some startling relationships emerge. Instead of many unrelated processing operations, you may see several groups of related processing operations. For example, if your business involves distribution of products, you may visualize a sales order processing group, including such elements as accounts receivable, inventory control, production planning (if you also manufacture your products), and shipping or traffic control. For a different kind of business, different groups (or set of groups) will appear, but appear they will. Each group (or, more properly, subsystem) can then be isolated for further analysis of its goal, its contribution to the goal of the over-all system, and its interaction with other subsystems in meeting that over-all goal. This process of *systems analysis* then descends to the next level of detail, and so on down through the ultimate details of processing within the area under study, always bringing to bear the perspective developed at the higher levels.

From one point of view, this system approach may sound trivial. After all, the relationships among elements of a current business data processing operation exist without any systems analysis. In fact, these relationships are inherent in the structure and organization of the company. However, what company can be certain that the relationships that grew up in a decentralized way are actually the best ones for meeting company goals? Systems analysis starts from a definition of those company goals served by information processing, and then evaluates the relationships and procedures for their contributions toward achieving them. Proceeding further, systems analysis investigates the values of improved or enlarged goals, balancing their values against the cost of achieving them. Those companies that have invested in a thorough systems analysis of their information processing operations have found that the study more than paid for itself, quite apart from the return on computerization that followed the study.

Because systems analysis requires definitions of over-all data processing goals, it is best performed by the top management of a company or in direct support of top management. In either case, management must understand this tool to make proper use of it, whether directly or in the hands of specialists. Accordingly, the bulk of this book discusses the system approach to management planning for, and use of, a computer. The chapters of this part are devoted to the computer as a business data processing system element, offering the perspectives needed for intelligent use of the computer, but avoiding unnecessary details.

2

WHAT IS A COMPUTER?

In its broadest sense, a computer is any system that can accept information, process it, and produce meaningful results. This definition is not very limiting because it covers not only the latest "giant brain" but also the lowliest clerk in an accounting or other business data processing operation. Generally, the term is used as an abbreviation for the unwieldy name "stored program electronic digital computer." If we examine the expanded name, we find first that a *digital* computer literally counts on its "fingers," or digits, working with numbers just as an adding machine does, whereas *analog* computers work with physical quantities representing other physical quantities. For example, a gasoline or fuel-oil metering pump is an analog computer, converting the volume of fuel delivered into turns of two wheels, one displaying price to the nearest cent and the other showing amount of fuel to the nearest tenth of a gallon. The digital computer, because it works with numbers, gives exact results (a cash register never shows a total between $4.11 and $4.11½), whereas an analog computer may give only approximate results. In a problem involving millions of dollars a digital computer can give answers correct to the cent (or even tenth of a cent, if needed), but an analog computer can answer only to the nearest hundred dollars.

An *electronic* computer can perform millions of elemental operations per second, in contrast to electromechanical calculators (e.g., cash registers, punched-card accounting machines), which can do only hundreds of operations per second. Even when electronic computer speed is reduced to lower its cost, the balance is in favor of the electronic computer; one computer, first used in 1960, cost no more than an equivalent punched-card machine system, yet operated some twenty times faster.

A *stored-program* computer offers greatest flexibility in its use, as well as maximum speed in each use. This stored program feature makes a computer a general-purpose device. By changing its program, a computer can be changed, say, from a cost accounting system to a sales order and inventory control system, and can be changed back, or it can be programmed for yet another application just as easily. Of equal importance, a stored program can be executed at the computer speed rather than at the speed of arrival of instructions from outside the computer. Finally, a stored-program computer can operate on its *program* (the sequence of instructions that directs its operations), modifying the sequence in accordance with the results of processing. This program modification capability allows the computer to make decisions; i.e., to select among alternate processing paths in its program, based on predetermined criteria established by the program.

COMPUTER STRUCTURE

A computer contains four functional elements or types of devices: memory or working storage, an arithmetic and logic (decision making) unit, a program control unit, and two or more input-output (I/O) devices. (The first three elements are often referred to as the central processing unit, or CPU.) An analogy best explains these units and their functions.

The arithmetic and logic unit is like a desk calculator; it can add, subtract, multiply, or divide two numbers at a time, and can perform many special operations for decision making (e.g., compare two numbers for equality or determine which is larger). The program control unit is the desk calculator "operator," faultlessly putting it through the operation sequence called for by the current program. Most of the computer I/O devices act as "in" and "out" baskets, supplying an item of input information on request from the "operator" and taking a processed output item for delivery outside the computer when the "operator" says it is ready.

Other, more or less specialized, I/O devices are used for file submission and updated file withdrawal, providing access to the fixed or slowly changing information needed by the "operator" (e.g., general ledger account records, current inventory, or payroll deduction schedules for the particular application).

In this analogy, the computer memory is the working desk space and scratch pad for the "operator," holding the item just taken from the "in" basket, the in-between results of processing, and the output information being readied for the "out" basket. In addition, the memory holds the computer program, the detailed "procedures manual" currently being followed by the computer "operator."

The computer most efficiently processes a large number of similar input items, taking one item at a time. For example, once its payroll processing program is loaded, the computer takes one time card and one master file record (for the same employee) into memory and performs all the processing for that transaction, including gross pay, deductions, net pay, etc., as well as updates the master file record (principally for year-to-date accumulations). The computer may also develop figures on overtime by department and by job, or just labor cost by job, issuing the results of these accumulations and others after all time cards have been processed. Once the processing for a particular time card is completed, output records are produced (e.g., a pay check and an updated master file record for that employee) and moved out of memory to one or more I/O devices. The computer then brings in the next time card and master file record to repeat its processing for this transaction, and so on until all time cards have been processed. The computer may then be loaded with a different program and different input and master files for some other processing operation.

In the example just given, if the computer "operator" is to cope with all varieties of time cards (e.g., piece rate, hourly, salaried, premium overtime, or shift incentive), its program, or "procedures manual," must anticipate and prescribe operations for all of them. As the number of variations increases, the program becomes larger, occupying more of the computer memory as well as costing more to prepare. In the event that the program becomes too large for the computer memory, it is divided into two or more smaller programs, each run separately on the computer to accomplish the complete processing operation (hence the name *run* for a separate portion of a complete operation). The number and variety of I/O devices used with the computer may also force division of a program into two or more runs. For example, a computer is usually equipped with only one line printer. Since payroll processing requires the printing of checks as well as a check register and job cost or overtime summary reports, it is usually split into two or more runs, with each run using the printer to produce a different output.

COMPUTER SPEED AND POWER

A computer is designed to perform a variety of elemental operations (e.g., add one number to another, or move an information item to a new position in memory). Each elemental operation is identified by a unique computer *instruction*, best visualized as the verb specifying that action. The *instruction list*, the complete set of different instructions, for a computer may number from forty to over a hundred items, depending upon the complexity of the computer. To perform a useful step in a processing operation, a string of these verbs (and their objects, called *addresses*) is developed by the programmer, each calling for the appropriate elemental operations often enough and in the right order for that step. For example, the computation of gross pay in a payroll processing program may require as many as a hundred elemental operations (not all different, of course). If the computer performs a million elemental operations per second, this gross pay calculation takes only 0.0001 second, quite fast but not so fast as the elemental operation time.

The number of different instructions that a computer can execute (the size of its instruction list) is not a good index of the speed or power of that computer; rather, it is an indication of the comparative ease in the programming of that computer. As you may have gathered from the example given above, of gross pay calculation, the computer speed in elemental operations may not give a good picture of its speed for any practical application. The elemental operation rate is a good, basic point of comparison between computers, but it does not tell the whole story. Differences in information organization, principally in computer memory, and in delivery rates between memory and the rest of the computer significantly modify the computer effective speed.

Visualize a computer memory as a series of pigeonholes (as in an old roll-top desk), each capable of holding one item of information. A computer memory may have anywhere from a thousand to a million of these pigeonholes, each having a unique address and each being equally accessible to the computer "operator." The size of a pigeonhole (and thus the basic information item size) may differ in different computers. This pigeonhole size can be likened to its "depth," measured in *bits*, the smallest possible unit of information. (A *bit* or binary digit may have either of two values, designated as "on" or "off": yes or no, or one or zero. Regardless of the designation chosen, two bits can represent four different items of information: both on, both off, first on and second off, or first off and second on. Three bits allow eight combinations and four bits cover sixteen combinations, and so on; n bits in a single information unit provide 2^n combinations and thus represent that many different items of information.)

The earliest business computers used pigeonholes that were 6 bits deep, each 6-bit combination representing one of 64 possible symbols, including the decimal digits 0 through 9, the 26 letters of the alphabet, and a variety of special symbols. (Actually, only 4-bit units were needed to accommodate the decimal digits 0 through 9, since a 4-bit unit has 16 different combinations. The two added bits are often called *zone bits*, a carry-over from punched-card terminology; with the two zone bits both valued at off or zero, the information is numeric, whereas zone bits valued at other than both zero identify the combination as alphabetic or some other symbol.) The 6-bit information unit in early models was called a *character* (letter, decimal digit, or some special symbol within the allowed set of 64), leading to the description of the computers that used this information unit (had character-sized pigeonholes) as character-organized.

In a character-organized computer, a 10-digit decimal number (e.g., 1152458580) occupies 10 pigeonholes. Adding it to another 10-digit number requires at least 30 unit-time intervals (the time interval for access to a pigeonhole), since three unit-time intervals are needed for each pair of digits. For example, one unit-time interval is needed to get the units digit of the number cited, another unit-time interval to get the units digit of the other number, and a third unit-time interval to store the sum digit in the units position. The same triplication is involved for the tens' digits, the hundreds' digits, and so on, exclusive of the unit-time intervals for access to the characters of the instruction that initiates the operation.

Other early computers used pigeonholes with a depth of from 12 to 64 bits, depending upon the computer in question. This pigeonhole depth defined the computer information unit which was called a *word* (because it contained more than one character).

Word-organized computers operate on one, two, or three words in each elemental operation (with memory delivering or accepting only one word during each unit-time interval). The addition of two numbers, each of which fits within a word, may thus require only three unit-time intervals (still ignoring the time for reading instructions) in contrast to the thirty unit-time intervals needed by a character-organized computer. In a word-organized computer, one unit-time interval brings out the first number, another unit-time interval brings out the second number, and the third unit-time interval puts the sum back into memory. (Additional unit-time intervals may be required for instruction reading, depending upon how many words or word locations a single instruction refers to.) A word-organized computer is thus faster than a corresponding (i.e., same unit-time interval or memory speed) character-organized computer, in the ratio of word size to character size. A word-organized computer is also usually larger and more expensive than a character-organized computer, in about the same ratio.

Many word-organized computers use binary arithmetic rather than the more familiar decimal arithmetic used by character-organized computers. A character-organized computer performs decimal arithmetic on *binary-coded decimal* (usually abbreviated as BCD) numbers. Each digit in a BCD number is represented by a 4-bit binary code (remember that 4 bits can represent as many as 16 different combinations, enough to cover the decimal digits 0 through 9). Addition of BCD numbers starts with addition of the units digits (in BCD form), then the tens' digits, then the hundreds' digits, and so on through the two numbers. Each 4-bit group is treated as a digit, and the weighting factor (units, tens, hundreds, etc.) changes as each successive group of 4 bits (i.e., each digit position) is handled. In binary notation, the extra positions are not thrown away (i.e., a 4-bit group can represent 0 through 15, not just 0 through 9). Instead, the 2^n combinations of n bits are assigned on a one-to-one basis to the decimal numbers from 0 through $2^n - 1$. In this notation, a 24-bit word can represent any number up to 16,777,215 ($2^{24} - 1$). By way of contrast, a character-organized representation using 24 bits can handle any number up to 9999; if the zone bits are stripped from this character-organized representation, any number up to 999,999 can be handled (in what is called *packed* BCD representation).

In all these cases, the sign of the number, whether plus or minus, has been ignored, something that is normally not possible; sign representation reduces binary notation in 24 bits to a maximum of 8,388,607 for binary, still 9.999 for unpacked BCD, and 99.999 for packed BCD. On the average, binary notation requires only 3.32 bits per decimal digit, in comparison to 6 bits per character or 4 bits per packed BCD digit (ignoring the additional bits for sign representation). Added to this economy in information representation for binary notation is the economy of uniform treatment in binary arithmetic; successive bit positions have uniformly increasing weighting factors (by 2), unlike the situation with BCD arithmetic where every fourth bit position requires a nonuniform weighting factor increase by 10. Of course information is normally submitted to any computer in the familiar decimal form, thus requiring a computer that uses binary arithmetic to convert input decimal data into binary form before it can be used internally, and similarly requiring conversion of binary results into decimal form for presentation as output. These conversion requirements have offset somewhat the economies of internal binary notation and arithmetic, but progressive simplifications of these conversion requirements have made the distinctions between internal decimal and internal binary operation less and less important.

In the mid-1960s, the computer industry reached a compromise between character- and word-organized computers by producing a new generation of "compatible" computers. This compromise may use a larger basic information unit, the *byte* (which is 8 bits deep, thus accommodating a full character or 2 BCD digits of 4 bits each in packed format), in place of the *character,* but operates in conjunction with word organization for greater speed in larger machines. The *byte* provides 256 different combinations, thereby expanding the computer alphabet to include both capital and small letters as well as many more special symbols. In these "compatible" computers, each pigeonhole (or addressable memory location) holds one byte. However, an instruction "verb" can address as its object(s) an adjacent pair of bytes (called a *half-word*), four adjacent bytes (called a *word*), or eight adjacent bytes (called a *double word*), depending upon the form of the instruction.

Basically, "compatible" computers operate with binary arithmetic on half-words, words, or double words (with different instructions for each size of information unit). They can also operate in decimal arithmetic on information fields of variable byte length, like character-organized computers. (Decimal arithmetic is an extra-cost option offered by some manufacturers, but is provided as standard equipment by others.)

Within a given line of compatible computers, all models offer the same organization and instruction list, thus allowing the programs written for one model to be executed on any other model in the line. The models differ in price, memory size, memory speed (or unit-time interval), and in the width of the data channel between memory and the rest of the computer. This data channel width determines how many bytes are delivered or accepted by memory during each unit-time interval. The smallest models offer a data channel width of one byte (exactly like character-organized computers); larger models have a data channel width of 4 bytes (a full word) and the largest models use a width of 8 bytes (a double word). As the data channel width increases, the speed and power of the computer increases, along with its cost. The over-all result of compatibility is that one computer can handle both business and engineering applications with provision for growth of these applications; a user can switch to a larger model in the same computer line without reprogramming his applications or retraining his personnel.

To summarize this discussion of computer speed and power, the effective speed of a computer on small scale depends on both its memory speed (or unit-time interval) and the size of the information unit in memory (character or word). This second factor is modified in the compatible lines of computers by the data channel width that determines the amount of information exchanged by the memory with other computer elements during any unit-time interval. On a larger scale, the power of a computer for any particular application depends strongly on its memory size (a larger memory allows single-run execution of longer programs) and on the number, variety, and efficiency of its I/O devices.

I/O DEVICES AND FILE HANDLING

Every computer requires *master files*, the storage of fixed or slowly changing information, to supplement its internal memory. The kinds of master files used with a particular computer depend on its size and application. The smallest current computers keep their files on punched cards or on magnetic cards. These computers are equipped with one or two card readers, a card punch or writer (which may include printing facilities), and a printer (a typewriter or a higher-speed device called a *line printer*). Small computers in this category are effective for short-cycle processing; e.g., credit card or utilities invoicing, and inventory updating. Other computers use a variety of specialized I/O devices for master file handling, making them more effective for longer processing cycles in more complex operations. These specialized I/O devices include magnetic tapes, magnetic drums, magnetic discs, and magnetic cards in large arrays, all of which will be discussed later in this chapter.

Any computer, after its program is loaded, processes one transaction record (e.g., weekly time card) at a time, applying the results of processing against the record from the master file affected by that transaction to update the file, and producing some output as a result of the transaction just processed (e.g., a pay check and an updated master file record). The complexity of the processing run on each transaction record is limited by the memory space left for the program after space has been allocated for input data (both transaction and master file records), output data, and intermediate processing results. The efficiency of the computer for a particular application depends on the balance between computing time and the time needed to move data into and out of memory via the I/O devices. When these times are roughly equal, the computer is running most efficiently and the run is said to be *balanced*. If these times are not equal, either the computer or its I/O devices are idle part of the time. When compute time is longer, the run is said to be *processor limited;* in the converse case, it is *I/O limited*.

In a card-only computer, the transaction records and the master file records must enter the computer through its card readers (preceded, of course, by the program). Since the computer reads cards in sequence from each source, the transaction records must be sorted into master file order before they can be submitted to the computer. (If the computer has only one reader, the transaction records must also be collated with the master file before submission.) Obviously, reading two or more cards to process each transaction takes longer than reading one card, disregarding the sorting time required before submission. Accordingly, many computers use additional I/O devices, usually faster than card readers, to enter programs and master file records. If these devices also use *sequential access* media like punched-card decks (e.g., magnetic tape), the transaction file must still be sorted into master file order before it is submitted. Only when the file storage device offers *random access* (i.e., approximately equal time of access for all records in a file) is the sorting requirement eliminated. Examples of random access devices include magnetic drums, magnetic discs, and magnetic cards in large arrays.

Random access I/O devices offer more than the elimination of presorting of transaction records. For example, in an inventory control application where 10 per cent of the items in inventory show 90 per cent of the activity, a computer with the master inventory file on a sequential medium (e.g., magnetic tape) will spend

90 per cent of its time on each update run in moving unaffected master file records from the current to the new master file. This relatively useless activity of collating transaction records with the few master file records affected on that run is eliminated entirely if the inventory file is stored in a random access device.

Of course, when a known segment of the inventory shows most of the activity, two master files can be set up to improve over-all efficiency. In this arrangement, one master file contains the active items; the other contains the remainder of the inventory items. Transaction records are correspondingly divided to match the file split and handled in separate processing runs, possibly performed at different intervals.

The gains from random access file storage become greater as master file size increases. In one application where the master file would have occupied 80 reels of magnetic tape, simply moving the master file through the computer for an update run would have taken over 4 hours; with the master file on a large random access storage device, a processing run that normally would affect only 5 per cent of the records would be completed in under 10 minutes. File splitting is not possible in this application because activity, although low, is distributed uniformly over the whole master file.

Random access I/O devices also allow the computer to perform *on-line* or demand processing instead of *batch* processing. In batch processing (the only form possible with sequential access devices), transaction records are accumulated either on a scheduled basis (e.g., weekly time cards) or on a quantity basis (e.g., 100 or 1000 records), then sorted, and submitted along with the program and appropriate master file. When processing of the batch is completed, the computer setup is "torn down" (i.e., the program and master file submission media and the results of processing are removed). After suitable setup, another batch (usually unrelated to the preceding one) is run on the computer. Batch processing can use random access storage devices to minimize presorting and to minimize copying of master file records, but for little else.

On-line or demand processing takes many forms, all of which require random access storage devices. One form avoids the assumed but unstated segregation of transaction records into different categories (e.g., inventory control, payroll, sales analysis). Instead, each transaction record identifies the processing it requires, thereby calling the appropriate program from random access storage into computer memory when that transaction record is entered. This form of on-line processing keeps each master file up to date on a minute-by-minute basis. Its cost varies with the number of categories of transactions processed and with the size of the processing programs. Although it may seem less efficient than batch processing because each transaction can require "teardown" and "setup," this form of demand processing can actually match or exceed the overall efficiency of batch processing by eliminating the batching delay. Furthermore, this form of demand processing is usually mixed with batch processing of naturally batched data (e.g., weekly time cards for payroll). In this mixed system, only high priority categories are processed on a demand basis, with the other categories of transaction records handled on a batch basis, either naturally or batched by the computer.

The purest mixed system provides demand processing of only one category of transactions; all other categories are handled in batches between servicing of demands. This form, sometimes described as a *query-response* system, is currently in use in airline reservations systems and in banking systems. In both cases, computers are used to accept queries from many different locations (reservations stations or teller windows) and to supply the necessary response to each query. An airline reservations clerk needs access to information about available seats on all his airline's flights for at least the next thirty days. He must also be able to reserve seats on any of these flights. Similarly, a bank teller must have access to information about any account at that bank and must be able to make changes to it.

In both cases, random access storage makes the required rapid access possible, yet these single-purpose on-line systems are much simpler than the multiple-purpose system described earlier. Rather than load and unload processing programs, the query-response system holds its query servicing program in computer memory, along with a traffic clerk program (sometimes called a *monitor*, or *executive*, or *supervisor* program). The traffic clerk examines each remote station in turn to determine whether it has requested service; if so, the servicing program is called to handle the station request and then return control to the traffic clerk. If the traffic clerk finds that time is available, after checking and servicing all pending requests, the system allows execution of a batch program in the interval before it must return to checking for queries from remote stations. As a result, the computer is kept fully occupied in servicing queries during peak load periods and filling in with batch processing (e.g., payroll) between queries in off-peak hours. This kind of multiple use of a computer is called *time sharing*, a term more comprehensive than immediately apparent because it covers any multiple use of a computer (including the multiple-category demand processing system described earlier), not just the mix of a single-purpose query-response system with batch processing.

Another term used interchangeably with *time sharing* is *multiprogramming*, more descriptive of the interleaving of two or more programs resident in memory at the same time and being executed together. The traffic clerk program is imperative in multiprogramming because it determines which resident program is to be executed at any given instant. The traffic clerk is called by each program to perform I/O operations. If a program must wait for completion of an I/O operation before it can proceed, the traffic clerk calls another program to proceed with execution while the first program is waiting for the end of its I/O operation, and conversely. The traffic clerk thus achieves a better balance between compute time and I/O time by averaging both over two or more programs.

Although many basic concepts have been presented in this discussion, it would not be complete without some treatment of the idea of *real-time* computer systems. The essential meaning of real time, here and now rather than at some point in an artificial time sequence, is simple but rather broad. Often, a query-response system like that for airline reservations is referred to as a real-time system, since each reservations clerk gets the impression that the computer is his direct servant (i.e., no apparent delay between query and response). In fact, the computer services many reservations clerks, giving each one the impression of immediate response.

These clerks are on-line to the computer, but they time-share its use: what is real time to them is artificial time to the computer. The term *real time* is better applied to computer systems that handle process control applications (e.g., oil refinery or continuous-flow chemical plants) or such things as air traffic control. In both cases, the computer must come up with answers rapidly enough for the answers to be useful rather than academic. For example, the answer to an airline pilot of, "You should have turned right two minutes ago," or the control signal to a valve in a refinery that arrives after several thousand gallons of partially converted crude have passed through but should have been diverted, these are academic answers because they are too late or in "unreal" time.

In general, a true real-time computer system handles only the real-time application; the computer is even hard-pressed to win and to continue winning its race with the clock in coming up with useful answers. The data in a real-time system is varying continuously and must be sampled at discrete intervals by the computer to develop a "true as of the previous instant" picture of the continuously varying process being controlled. Analog computers, with their ability to deal simultaneously and continuously with many variables, were and are used extensively in real-time, process-control applications. Digital computers use speed to compensate for their one-at-a-time treatment of input variables, but offer long-term accuracy that exceeds what is available from analog computers. Demand and query-response computer systems offer real-time performance to their users on a human time scale; the answers are "here and now" to the user. This sense of real time is, however, a far cry from its sense in continuous or process control applications.

To summarize this wide-ranging discussion, realize that a card-only computer offers only low-speed entry points for data and master file records. These sequential access entry points restrict the computer to batch processing of input records that are sorted into master file order before submission. The addition of a faster sequential I/O device (or devices) for master file handling will speed processing but still requires sorting of transaction records, before submission, into master file order. The addition or substitution of random access I/O devices allows the submission of unsorted transaction records (in a single category) for batch processing or the use of on-line processing (demand or query-response) of high-priority items together with batch processing of naturally batched or lower priority items. On-line processing can vary in complexity from query-response systems (single-category demand processing with batch processing of all other categories) through multiple-category demand systems, both mixed with batch processing. True real-time or process control systems differ from these approaches in that they are fully occupied by their application and race with the clock ("On the signal, begin your descent to 20,000 feet.").

I/O MEDIA AND THEIR CHARACTERISTICS

After the foregoing discussion of the two general classes of I/O devices (sequential and random access), a survey of the I/O media and their characteristics is in order. The characteristics in question include cost, capacity, data transfer rate, and average access time (how long does the computer wait before it gets the record it has requested?) for random access media. The standard for comparison is the computer memory—the most costly, fastest, and most random medium of storage available. In terms of monthly rental charges, additional computer memory capacity costs from $17 to $51 per thousand characters or bytes. Data transfer rates run from 87,000 characters per second (11.5 microseconds per character) up through 4,000,000 characters (or words, which are larger) per second (0.25 microsecond per character or word), with capacities from 1000 characters to over a million. Access time for computer memories is about one-quarter of their unit-time intervals, ranging from about 4 microseconds down through 0.6 microsecond. Obviously, cost increases with speed and size of the information unit (character, byte, or word).

Computer memory is not, properly, an I/O device, but some manufacturers now offer add-on mass memory devices as I/O units. These units are, in general, slower than the internal computer memories (8 microseconds unit-time interval compared with 2 or 1 microsecond for internal memory). These stand-alone or add-on memories cost from $56 to $168 per month per thousand bytes, offer capacities of millions of bytes, and have transfer rates of about 120,000 bytes per second. (Word organization and wider data channels increase this rate and the cost as well.)

Punched Cards

Turning from the "top of the line," consider now the workhorse I/O medium of the computer field, the punched card. A single punched card in the most popular format can hold a maximum of 80 characters. (See Figure 1.) Card stock costs about $1.00 per

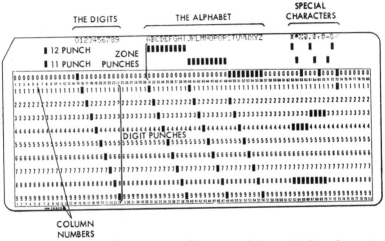

Courtesy of International Business Machines Corporation

Figure 1. Common Punched Card

thousand (without special printing on the cards), but the expenses of key punching and verifying the data entered on cards add about $23 to that figure. Punched cards can be read by computer input devices at rates from 100 to 3000 cards per minute, with the slower readers being cheaper. (To convert rates from cards per minute to characters per second, multiply by 80/60, or 4/3.)

Punched cards are used for file storage and resubmission, but computer punching rates of from 80 to 300 cards per minute (with a cost differential for the different speeds) limit their use to low-volume or low-speed applications. Punched cards are strictly sequential, so access time is too long to be useful unless a multiple card-feed system is coupled to the processor. In all but card-only computers, punched cards are used principally for submission of low-volume transactions. They may be produced as output by a computer for *turnaround* applications in which a computer-originated document returns to the processing system as an input that requires no key punching (e.g., credit card or utilities invoice).

Perforated Tape

Perforated tape is similar to punched cards in being a sequential medium, but it offers some advantages as an I/O medium for computers. First, perforated tape can be produced as a by-product of some manual operations (e.g., on cash registers, TWX, or Telex*, several calculating typewriters), thus providing computer-readable data without the extra expense of key punching. Most current computers will accept data in ASCII (American Standards Code for Information Interchange) code on perforated tape. Since TWX and Telex services using ASCII code are available, data from remote locations can be sent to the computer center for recording on computer-compatible perforated tape and subsequent direct submission to the computer. The computer can also prepare output data on perforated tape for automatic transmission to the originating point.

A second advantage of perforated tape is that it will accommodate records longer than 80 characters, the capacity of a single punched card. These long records become more expensive on punched cards because each additional card must use some space for an identification field, associating this "trailer" card with the "header" card of the record. On the other hand, punched card records are easier to correct than are perforated tape records; an erroneous punched card can be removed and replaced by a correct card, whereas a perforated tape record must be spliced or repunched to replace an error.

A third advantage is that perforated tape records can be read at

---

* TWX and Telex are registered trademarks of, respectively, the American Telephone and Telegraph Company and the Western Union Telegraph Company.

up to 1000 characters per second (equivalent to 750 cards per minute) with equipment that is cheaper than the card readers of comparable speed. (Lower-speed perforated tape readers are correspondingly cheaper.) Normal output speeds for perforated tape are about 100 characters per second (comparable to 75 cards per minute), although higher-speed perforators are available at significantly higher cost. Perforated tape output is also harder to verify than is the corresponding punched card output.

Finally, perforated tape records can now be sorted by account or item numbers, a capability limited originally to punched card records.

Pin-punched Tickets

Continuing this catalog of I/O media, pin-punched tickets or tags (produced by Kimball or Dennison) are used by some department stores for sales analysis and inventory control. These midget punched cards, with smaller than common holes, are usually machine-read for conversion into punched cards, but some reading equipment can be used to submit these tags directly to a computer without the conversion step. Pin-punched tags are not widely used as I/O media because they offer some difficulty in machine reading; they are included in this survey for completeness.

MICR and OCR

Two other I/O media are worth considering together; MICR (Magnetic Ink Character Recognition) and OCR (Optical Character Recognition). Both media use machine-readable symbols instead of punches on a cardlike document. (There are some exceptions to this cardlike document prescription for OCR, discussed later.) The most widespread use of MICR is on bank checks, employing the slightly odd-looking numbers and special symbols printed across the bottom of each check. These MICR symbols (collectively described as the E-13B font) were developed for the American Banking Association to automate check handling, but they are usable for other purposes that can be satisfied by the decimal digits 0 through 9 and four other symbols. (See Figure 2.)

Printing and imprinting costs for MICR are comparable to punched-card costs. Currently, the equipment for reading and sorting of MICR documents is much more costly than punched-card equipment, but this cost should decrease as more equipment of this

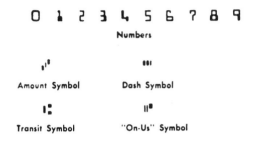

Numbers

Amount Symbol   **Dash Symbol**

Transit Symbol   **"On-Us" Symbol**

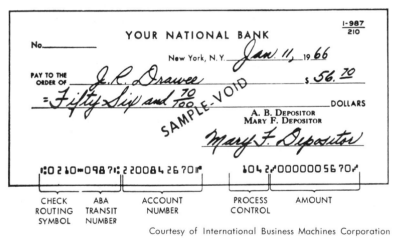

Courtesy of International Business Machines Corporation

Figure 2. MICR Characters and Application

type is designed and put into use.

Optical Character Recognition (OCR) is widely used currently in credit card systems that employ manual embossed-plate imprinters. (However, even now, cash registers are available with OCR tape outputs for direct submission to computers.) Most gasoline

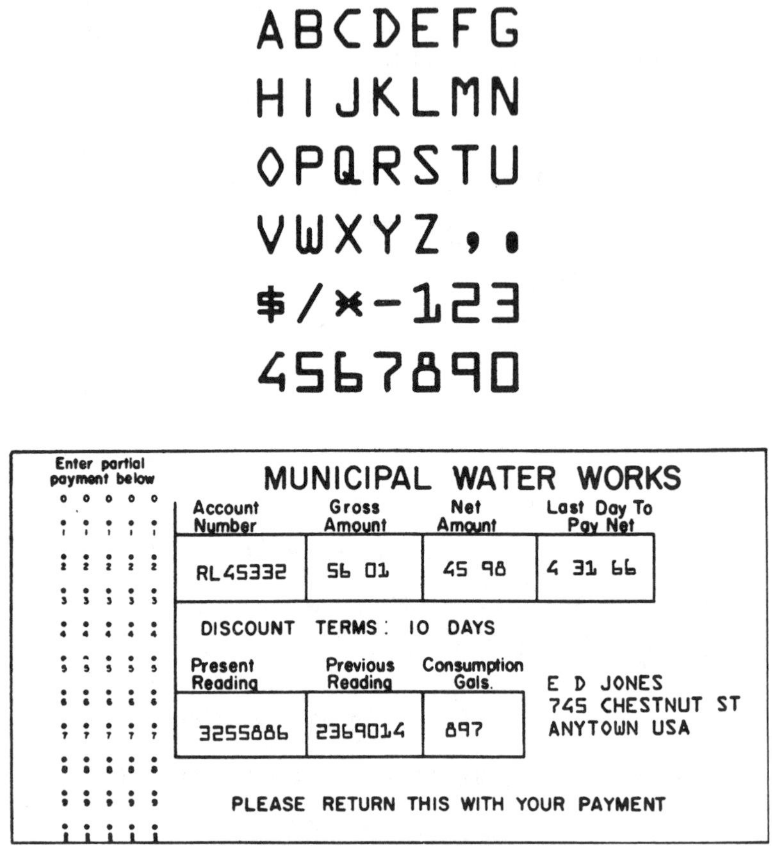

ABCDEFG
HIJKLMN
OPQRSTU
VWXYZ,.
$/*-123
4567890

Enter partial payment below	MUNICIPAL WATER WORKS			
o o o o o : : : : : : : : : : : : : : :	Account Number	Gross Amount	Net Amount	Last Day To Pay Net
: : : : : : : : : :	RL45332	56 01	45 98	4 31 66
: : : : : : : : : :	DISCOUNT TERMS : 10 DAYS			
: : : : : : : : : :	Present Reading	Previous Reading	Consumption Gals.	E D JONES
: : : : : : : : : :	3255886	2369014	897	745 CHESTNUT ST ANYTOWN USA
: : : : : : : : : : : : : : :	PLEASE RETURN THIS WITH YOUR PAYMENT			

Courtesy of International Business Machines Corporation

Figure 3. OCR Characters and Application

credit cards, for example, are plastic plates bearing the holder's account number in boxy-looking characters. These numbers imprinted on each transaction record are designed for machine reading. (See Figure 3.)

In some applications, OCR data is submitted directly to a computer; however, most credit card systems use an OCR reader and card punch combination to convert the record into a punched card. The unit punches the OCR-recorded account number automatically; an operator then reads the amount of the charge and keys it in to be punched on the same card. The transaction record, carrying account number and amount, is then processed by punched-card equipment or by a computer.

Embossed-plate imprinters for OCR recording, including amount imprinting from manually set controls, cost under $100. Rental costs for the reader-punch combinations are comparable to the cost of a key punch unit plus operator. A keyboard unit like a cash register can be obtained with OCR output capability for little more than the basic cost of the unit itself; conversion of an existing unit for OCR recording is considerably more expensive. OCR readers for continuous recordings (like cash register tapes) are not, unfortunately, very cheap. However, most computer manufacturers offer conversion services, which are billed on a volume basis.

These costs must, of course, be compared with the costs of other methods for conversion of data into machine-readable form. As a parting note, much work is being done on machine reading of handwritten numbers and letters; this work is promising in its ability to handle run-of-the-mill handwriting (or rather hand printing), but it is still in the testing stage as this is written.

High-Speed Media

Having covered all low-cost sequential I/O media (except for one, the magnetic card, explained later), let's now turn to the high-speed, high-volume media that are used more for file storage than for submission of transaction records. All these media use magnetic recording similar to that used for sound and television recording (and similar, too, to the recording technique of computer memory, which is also magnetic). The differences among these media derive from the form in which the magnetic material is used, that is, long narrow strips or much shorter and wider loops or closed bands.

MAGNETIC TAPE—The form of magnetic recording most widely used by computers has been magnetic tape. A magnetic-tape reel of the standard type costs about $25, can hold up to 23 million characters, and can be read or written on (by an appropriate tape drive unit) at from 15,000 to 340,000 characters per second. Magnetic tape is almost a purely sequential medium, since each character (or byte) is recorded on a line across the width of the tape, successive characters (or bytes) of a record are recorded in sequence along the length of the tape, and successive records are also arranged along the length of the tape but separated by unrecorded gaps between them. (See Figure 4.) It is possible to skip over a record or group of records to achieve some degree of random access to records. However, a high-speed tape drive takes about 4 minutes to pass through a full reel of tape, making the average access time 2 minutes or more.

The cost of magnetic tape use is not, of course, limited to the cost of the tape reels. Computer tape drives rental ranges from $110 to $760 per month, depending upon their versatility and speeds. Normally, one tape drive unit is not enough (except in some low-speed applications where a single tape drive unit is used to store and retrieve large blocks of data that have overflowed computer memory and the associated random access device). In most magnetic-tape applications, a single pass through a tape reel either reads the tape or writes on it, almost never both. Thus, if a magnetic-tape drive is used to submit master file records (reading them into the computer), another tape drive unit is needed to record on the new master file reel those records unaffected by transaction records and those updated records produced by processing. In addition, a third tape drive is necessary to introduce the processing program, unless time is allowed to recopy the processing program from the old master file tape onto the new one. On top of this multiplication of tape drives is the requirement for a tape control unit to coordinate the tape drives with the computer.

Certain advantages accrue from this multiplication of tape drives. First, with three tape drives, the computer can sort input records (after they have been put onto magnetic tape), thus removing the need for punched-card or perforated-tape sorters. Three tape drives are the minimum for sorting; as the number increases, sorting speed increases, since fewer passes from tape to tape are needed. Second, as more tape drives are provided with a

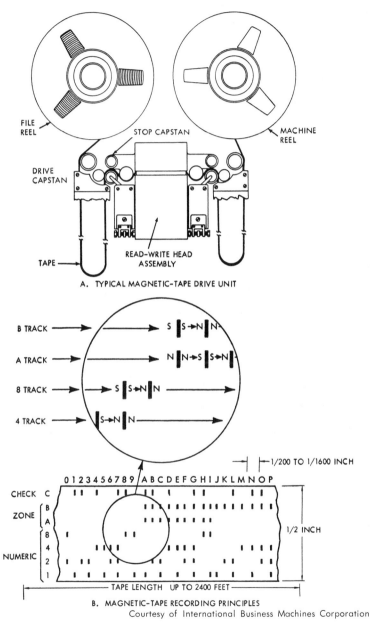

FILE REEL

STOP CAPSTAN

MACHINE REEL

DRIVE CAPSTAN

READ–WRITE HEAD ASSEMBLY

TAPE

A. TYPICAL MAGNETIC-TAPE DRIVE UNIT

B TRACK → S |S→N| N

A TRACK → N |N→S| S→N|

8 TRACK → S |S→N| N →

4 TRACK → |S→N| N →

1/200 TO 1/1600 INCH

0 1 2 3 4 5 6 7 8 9 A B C D E F G H I J K L M N O P

CHECK   C

ZONE { B
        A

         8
NUMERIC 4
         2
         1

1/2 INCH

TAPE LENGTH   UP TO 2400 FEET

B. MAGNETIC-TAPE RECORDING PRINCIPLES

Courtesy of International Business Machines Corporation

Figure 4. Magnetic-Tape Recording

computer, the scheduling of batch processing can be tightened, since the next batch can be set up on inactive tape drives while the current batch is using other tape drives. As a point of interest, large computers are designed to accommodate as many as 40 tape drives; very large computers can accommodate up to 256 tape drives.

MAGNETIC DRUMS—All other magnetic recording media, which offer random access capabilities unlike magnetic tape, can be visualized as special arrangements of magnetic tape. A magnetic drum is equivalent to a series of tape strips wrapped side by side around a cylinder, with a read-write head for each tape strip. (See Figure 5.) To select a given strip (or *track*, as it is usually called), the read-write head above it is selected electronically. Access time then is the time required for the item to be read (or the position to be written) to arrive under the selected head. Average access time, defined as one-half the period of drum revolution, ranges from 1/10 to 1/100 second for most drums, as determined by their rate or rotation. Capacities range upward into the millions of characters (or bytes), depending on drum size.

The data transfer rate varies with the organization of the drum. A word-organized drum (each read-write head accommodates a word at a time, or each strip or track is wider than a character or byte) approaches computer memory speed; in fact, drums were used as computer memories before magnetic-core memories were developed. Character or byte organization of a drum gives the same transfer rate, but for smaller information units (like the diminished data channel width of small compatible computers); thus it is effectively slower, but cheaper as well. Drum storage is probably the most flexible of all random access storage media, offering three means of controlling reading or writing, or both: by address (as in computer memory), by status (is the slot empty or full?), and by identity (does the item match the search key?). For example, one MICR bank check system writes the account number and amount from each check onto a drum by status. The randomly ordered entries are then read by identity against an ascending account number key to get the items into account number order.

Drum storage costs depend strongly on the information unit size (character, byte, or word) and on the degree of versatility included

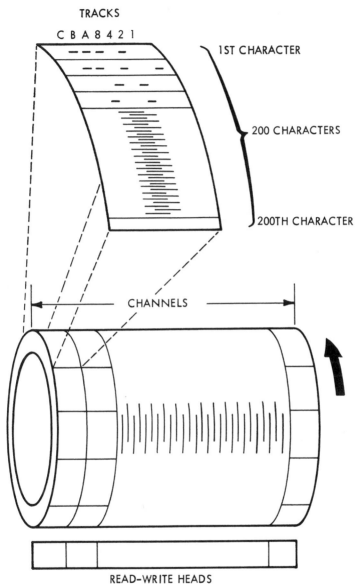

TRACKS

C B A 8 4 2 1

1ST CHARACTER

200 CHARACTERS

200TH CHARACTER

CHANNELS

READ–WRITE HEADS

Courtesy of International Business Machines Corporation

Figure 5. Magnetic-Drum Recording

in the reading and writing controls for the drum. A byte-organized drum may cost from 1.3 cents to $52 per month per thousand bytes without any special degrees of versatility beyond reading or writing by address.

MAGNETIC DISCS—Magnetic-disc storage is similar in most ways to

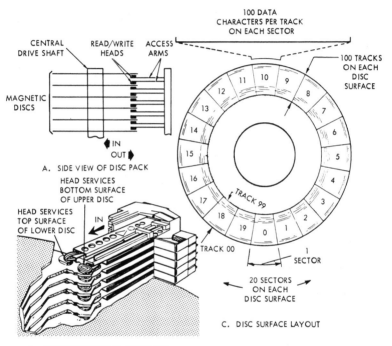

Courtesy of International Business Machines Corporation

Figure 6. Magnetic-Disc Recording

drum storage. Since only the surface of a medium is used for magnetic recording, discs of the same over-all dimensions as a drum provide more surface within the same volume. Disc storage units thus carry a set of discs like a juke box (although some disc storage units use one oversized disc, which may or may not be changeable manually). Each disc surface is divided into a set of tracks, each wide enough to accommodate a character or byte across its width. (See Figure 6.) All tracks on one surface, in turn, are divided into sectors or pie wedges, each sector portion of a track holding a fixed number of characters or bytes, usually 100 or 200. Each sector of each track on each disc surface is separately addressable (like each pigeonhole in computer memory).

In some disc storage units, there is only one read-write head on each arm for each disc surface (two heads per arm, since the arm moves between two surfaces). In these units, the arms, moving like a comb between the discs, must be indexed mechanically to select a track. In this case, access time includes two elements: the time required to move the arms and the time needed by the addressed sector to arrive under the heads. (The time for electronic selection of a disc surface is negligible compared with the times for mechanical indexing and sector arrival.) In other disc storage units, each arm carries a read-write head for every track it has access to, thus making it unnecessary to move the arms unless the discs are changed. Access times vary from 1/100 second up to 4/5 second with different disc storage units. Capacities range up to 200 million characters or bytes in the larger units. Costs vary with speed and size from 3½ cents to 13 cents per thousand characters per month.

As mentioned above, some disc storage units have replaceable discs or disc packs, giving random access to the contents of each changeable set but sequential access to successive sets. A disc pack may cost up to $250; large, single discs used with a "manual player" unit are usually cheaper. The capacity of a changeable set varies from 2 to 55 million bytes, depending on its design.

MAGNETIC-CARD ARRAYS—Still larger storage capacity is offered by magnetic cards in large arrays. Magnetic cards can be visualized as strips of magnetic tape mounted side by side on long cards. A group of cards is held in a magazine, one of several in the magnetic-card-handling unit. (See Figure 7.) When a card is addressed, its magazine is moved into position (if not already there) to have access to the cards inside. The addressed card is then selected mechanically from the magazine, loaded onto a cylinder, and spun past a set of read-write heads. The whole unit thus acts like a magnetic drum with many changeable surfaces.

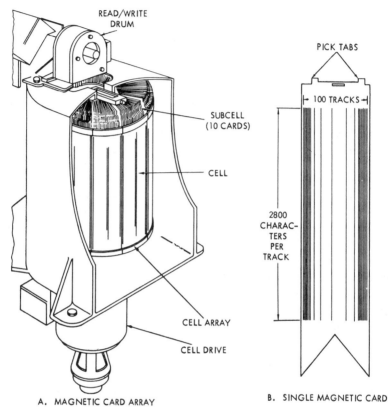

A. MAGNETIC CARD ARRAY   B. SINGLE MAGNETIC CARD

Courtesy of International Business Machines Corporation

Figure 7. Magnetic-Card Array

For economy, the read-write station may have only one set of heads, which are indexed mechanically across the width of the card to select the addressed strip or track. Access time from card to card ranges up to 1 second, with most of that time spent in magazine movement and card selection. On a single card, access time is about 1/30 second.

Data transfer rates are comparable to magnetic-tape rates. Capacities of a single card array vary from five million up to two billion characters or bytes; these capacities can be increased by using multiple arrays or, with sequential access, by changing magazines. (A magazine may cost as much as $250.) Magnetic-card arrays offer storage costs of from 8 cents to 11 cents per thousand characters per month, decreasing as installed capacity approaches the maximum capacity of the array.

LOW-SPEED MAGNETIC CARDS—On a much smaller scale, the magnetic card is also used as a sequential access medium by some small computers and bookkeeping equipment. A magnetic card the size of a punched card can hold up to 900 characters (less in some designs), as compared with 80 on a punched card. These magnetic cards thus offer up to a tenfold increase in data transfer rate over punched cards, yet at comparable equipment costs.

Some small computers use a magnetic card reader-writer to handle master file records, and another device (punched-card reader, perforated-tape reader, or even a manual keyboard) is used to submit transaction records. Some bookkeeping systems use ledger cards with magnetic stripes on their backs. The stripe carries the account number, current line for entry, and current balance in machine-readable form. When the ledger card is inserted, it is positioned automatically at the first line for new entry. The account number read from the card is compared with that keyed in by the operator, to assure that the entry applies against that record. The entry is then allowed, printed on the face of the card, and applied to update the current balance and record the new figure on the magnetic strip.

Graphic Output Media

Two I/O media have been ignored so far in this survey: the line printer and the variety of special output display devices that are used with computers (e.g., television type of display, graph plotter). The *line printer*, so-called because it prints a whole line in a single step, produces the bulk of computer output that is used away from the computer; it is the basic delivery point for computer-prepared reports.

Line printers vary in speed from 90 to 1500 lines per minute (maximum speed, that is; effective speeds vary with the application). Their line width may also differ, ranging from 80 to 144 letters and spaces per line. The cost of a line printer increases with line width and speed as well as with the number of different characters it can print. Most line printers offer a standard set of 48 different characters (letters, numbers, punctuation marks, and some special symbols); some printers may use 64 different characters and still others may be expanded up to 128 different characters (to accommodate both capital and small letters, for example).

The only possible alternative to a line printer with a medium or large computer is a *page printer*, a device that produces the equivalent of 150,000 lines per minute at a correspondingly higher cost. Their high cost limits page printers to very high volume applications. Several military departments have used page printers for output of computer-prepared supply catalogues running over 10,000 pages, realizing considerable savings by releasing their computer for other work. Page printers are versatile as well as fast. One recent use of a page printer was in a computerized reapportionment of voting districts. The page printer not only printed the report but also drew the maps of the voting districts. Again, most manufacturers of page printers and some computer rental facilities offer the use of these devices on a part-time basis for conversion from magnetic tape form to graphic form.

Very small computers may use an electric typewriter in place of a line printer, for economy, but electric typewriter speed is low, ranging from 15 to 40 characters per second (equivalent to 11 to 30 lines per minute for full lines). Obviously, this low speed limits the volume of graphic output that the computer can produce efficiently. Larger computers also use electric typewriters, but only for direct communication with humans. For example, the typewriter included in a computer control console is used to alert the operator to conditions that require his attention, such as mounting and dismounting tape reels.

Other Output Display Devices

The other output display devices used with computers are of limited use in pure batch processing, yet are essential for on-line processing (either full demand or query-response). For example, the bank teller query-response system equips each teller window with a television type of display unit and a keyboard. The teller enters a depositor's account number on the keyboard, causing a display of that current balance. When the teller keys in a transaction, it may also be displayed for his verification before the computer accepts it to update the account. This type of display unit is rather expensive, although prices decline as the number of units increases; a single unit may rent for as much as $400 a month. As a result, until cheaper display units become available, many systems use electric typewriters or teletypewriters instead. In an adaptation of the banking system described above, instead of flashing the balance immediately on a screen, an electric typewriter takes a second or so to type it out.

Other, more specialized output devices such as graph plotters are not in general use in business data processing systems because their cost is not justified by the volume of output required from them. Ordinary line printers can produce bar graphs very easily (line graphs are much more difficult, but still possible), and graph plotters are available for part-time use to handle occasional heavy loads.

To conclude this survey of I/O media, computers equipped only with low-speed sequential I/O devices (such as punched-card reader-punches, perforated-tape equipment, or magnetic-card reader-writers) are limited to batch processing and short-run operations. The addition or substitution of high-speed sequential access devices (such as magnetic-tape drives) increases the over-all processing speed, but still restricts the system to batch processing. Random access storage devices can improve the efficiency of batch processing (e.g., of large files with low but distributed activity), but are more important in allowing demand processing.

As the costs of random access devices come down (and the savings on data conversion in demand systems are recognized along with the value of up-to-the-minute file currency), demand processing will be used more widely in smaller computer applications. These applications will use demand processing of almost all categories of transactions, using random access storage for the necessary programs and master files. Some transactions such as daily time reports will be sorted and edited in random access storage, then shifted as blocked data to magnetic tape to be batched for the weekly payroll run. As a result, the system will time-share demand processing with batch processing. Since the compatible computers discussed earlier require the use of a *supervisor* or traffic clerk program, they are directly suited for these mixed applications that best use the computer and its I/O devices.

3

WHAT IS A COMPUTERIZED
DATA PROCESSING SYSTEM?

A computerized data processing system requires more than a computer for its operation. The system must include facilities for input data collection and conversion into machine-readable form. The system must also provide the computer with programs and must accommodate changes to those programs. Above all, the system must include administration to schedule its operation and to coordinate the activities of the system elements to meet that schedule. These system elements will be considered separately in this chapter.

INPUT DATA COLLECTION AND CONVERSION

In every batch processing system, there is a room full of key punches, used to transcribe source documents onto punched cards (or equivalent equipment for conversion onto perforated tape). In addition to the key punches are usually verifiers, machines like key punches but which read punched cards and compare them with the same information being entered on the keyboard. Of course there must be key punch operators, verifier operators, and usually a supervisor.

In another room, and usually not a part of the computer system, source document editors establish the completeness and acceptability of each source document, sort the documents into batches, and establish controls for each batch. The batch control validates the completeness and accuracy of the processing by the computer system (including the key punching and verifying) for that batch. Although source document editing may not be identified formally in a manual system, the function is performed. For example, in a manual inventory control system, the stock clerk performs a source document edit each time he examines an inventory request for completeness and validity. In a computerized inventory control system, the stock clerk usually continues to perform this edit function. However, an additional edit may be required to simplify key punching and to establish batch controls. This additional edit can be avoided if the inventory request form is redesigned for key punching convenience and the stock clerk originates the batch-control. In this example, the batch control might be a bogus inventory charge of the total number of items issued that day, assuming the day's transactions are handled as a batch. Of course, if the inventory control application were handled by a demand processing system, batch control and even transcription of inventory change documents onto punched cards would be unnecessary.

For batch processing, transcription onto punched cards (or other machine-readable medium) is almost inevitable if the source documents originate outside the control of the company processing them. Further, these documents are likely to require considerable editing if they are in free form; i.e., if the order of information on a source document varies widely from that desired for key punching. This problem is reduced by mail-order firms who supply printed order forms to their customers; they thereby get most of their orders in the desired form, minimizing the number of orders that require heavy editing. Other companies face this problem by reducing the over-all cost of data conversion. Following their edit of source documents, these companies perform limited processing that also converts the source documents on a by-product basis. For example, a sales order processing application for a regional parts distributor uses typewriters with limited computing capability to prepare a multipart form from each edited source document. The multipart form includes an invoice and a shipping list among other things. The computing typewriter not only extends the price on each order item and totals the order, but also prepares a perforated-tape record of the source document for use in computer sales analysis. Thus, the keyboard operation accomplishes worthwhile processing and the conversion for submission to a computer.

Other methods of data conversion are possible when the source documents are originated within the company. Forms can be designed for ease in key punching, or data can be captured closer to its source in machine-readable form. In the second case, the conversion function is effectively decentralized and incorporated into other operations at no added cost; the edit function is either eliminated or divided between the document originator and the computer. One lunch-counter chain in New York City uses mark-sense cards (cards marked in specified areas with a special pencil for automatic punching) as customer checks. These cards, also imprinted by the cash register with the total amount collected, are used in inventory control and sales analysis by the store. These mark-sense cards, with their limited information capacity, are sufficient to handle the restricted menu of this chain.

In other applications, prepunched cards are returned as source documents for computer processing. Many credit card and utility invoicing systems use this technique, called *turnaround*. The invoice form carries a payment stub for return by the customer, which is prepunched with account number and amount due. Upon receipt, the payment is checked against the amount due; if they match, the payment stub is submitted as a source document, recording receipt of payment; if they do not match, a new card is prepared. The *turnaround* technique is also used with punched cards for inventory control or with pin-punched tickets for department stores sales analysis. In both cases, the prepunched card or pin-punched ticket is returned as a source document when the inventory item is charged out or the department store item is sold.

Still another approach to input data collection and conversion uses data collection devices at the document origination points to record data on punched cards, perforated tape, or on magnetic tape (whether computer-compatible or not). OCR cash register tapes also fall into this category. The data collected at each station in machine-readable form is picked up regularly for batch submission to the computer. Data collection devices vary widely in capacity, features, and costs (from a purchase price of $60 for an OCR embosser like those used in credit-card transaction recording, on up). They all record data at their source in machine-readable form, thus avoiding or minimizing the cost of subsequent data conversion.

The use of data communications facilities (TWX, Telex, or Data-Phone* service) allows the rapid movement of data from remote points, combined with their conversion into machine-readable form. In a demand processing system, the data communications facilities must be "on-line" (i.e., directly connected) to the computer; for batch processing, the terminal at the computer site need only accumulate incoming data. The simplest data communications network uses TWX (Bell System) or Telex (Western Union) service between the originating stations and the computer site. (If the communications network is within one building, the terminal units can be rented and connected together by in-plant wiring, rather than going through the dial network and paying toll charges.) The keyboarding of source documents is transmitted via the common carrier at from 65 to 100 words per minute or higher (a word here is defined as six characters). These data may then enter the computer directly or be received on perforated tape for later submission. The costs for this service include monthly rental charges on the terminal units and the toll charges on each transmission, determined by distance and duration.

As the transmission distance increases for a particular volume of data, the toll charges increase to a point where higher speed transmission over voice-grade channels becomes competitive. Voice-grade transmission via Bell System's Data-Phone (or similar facilities offered by Western Union and by independent telephone companies) allows speeds up to 2,500 words per minute on dial telephone lines, thus cutting the duration of transmission by a factor of 25 or so. To use these high speeds, the keyboarding must be done

---

* TWX and Data-Phone are registered trademarks of the American Telephone and Telegraph Company; Telex is registered by the Western Union Telegraph Company.

"off-line" from the transmission channel; the converted data are then read into the Data-Phone by another unit. At the receiving end, another Data-Phone presents the received data for recording or direct entry into the computer. In either case, additional equipment is required over that for TWX or Telex, but this additional cost is offset by the toll charge savings over long enough distances and large enough data volumes.

Although data communications may seem too costly for small business data processing systems, its costs must be compared with the savings it offers in decentralized input conversion and in speedy data presentation for processing at a central location. One office supplies company found it profitable to equip each of its major customers with its catalogue in punched-card form, a small hand-fed card reader with a numeric keyboard, and a Data-Phone. When a customer wishes to place an order, he dials the office supplies company on his Data-Phone and identifies his company by feeding a prepunched identity card into the reader. He then feeds into the reader the card describing the first item he wishes to order. On signal that the card has been transmitted, he keys in the quantity requested, then feeds in the next item card, and so on through his entire order. At the receiving end, an automatic key punch connected to the Data-Phone produces a set of cards describing the complete order. These cards are entered into sales order processing without delay for edit or conversion. The office supplies company pays $10 a month for the card reader and $40 a month for the Data-Phone on each customer's premises. It has found that the increase in sales to these customers (double or triple its previous volume from them) more than offsets these fixed costs. Savings on clerical costs are an additional gain in this application.

Until recently, the cheapest and most reliable data transmission method was the U.S. Post Office, but rising postal costs and the inevitable delay of one to two days is making the advantage questionable. (Another often overlooked method for moving data rapidly between cities is the express service offered by long-haul passenger bus lines.) When these delays become too costly or the dangers of losing data that leaves your premises become too great, other data transmission methods should be investigated with the cooperation of the utilities that offer them. Even when there is no problem of moving data from remote locations to a central processing location within a company, data communications can be useful in other ways. From a reverse viewpoint, a small company that cannot justify full-time use of a computer may use a data communications link to a computer rental facility. The company pays only for the time it uses on the computer, and avoids the problem of moving possibly irreplaceable records off its premises (physically, that is). With direct access to the computer, also, no one has access to these records even at the computer center.

As of 1966, ten computer rental facilities are offering time-shared access to their computers via data communications links, with this number likely to grow (although some of these facilities serve only members of a trade organization). One facility specializes in small science-engineering problems, offering the user a dialogue with the computer. A user must spend roughly $165 per month for a terminal unit and a Data-Phone plus $325 per month for a minimum of 25 hours of computer time (telephone toll charges are extra). Other facilities handle both science-engineering problems and business applications. Invoice preparation charges are 7½ cents per invoice plus 2½ cents per line on an invoice; there are also fixed monthly charges for master file and program storage as well as for the data communications terminal. Other computer rental facilities offer non–time-shared (i.e., batch processing) access to their computers at somewhat lower cost. A data communication link moves the input data to the computer center and after processing returns the results to the user. Since batch processing at the computer center allows scheduling at its convenience, the user suffers some delay (usually no longer than overnight) along with the advantage of economy.

An interesting sidelight to the marriage of data communications with the computer is the use of data communications to shift around processing loads when a computer is overloaded or down for maintenance. The communications-equipped computer center simply transmits the data to be processed (and the processing program) to the backup computer center by dialing its Data-Phone number.

To summarize this discussion of input data collection and conversion, the equipment and efforts needed to "feed" a computer with input data form a significant cost element beyond that of the computer itself. With pure batch processing and uncontrollable "free form" source documents, centralized source document editing and conversion is almost inevitable. The costs of this centralization can be reduced (in low-volume operations) by making conversion a by-product of useful processing outside the computer. Over-all costs are reduced further by decentralizing the data conversion operation, capturing input data in machine-readable form at or as near to the source as possible. (The data originator is also its best editor if procedures have been defined and checks are made by the computer.) One simple technique for input data capture uses computer-prepared source documents (sometimes called *turnaround*) such as prepunched cards and pin-punched tickets. This technique or the use of data collection devices is suitable for batch processing. Data communications (either solely in-plant or including remote points) is essential for demand processing, but can also be useful in batch processing, to minimize delays while doing conversion into machine-readable form.

TWX or Telex service is most economical for low-volume, short-distance communication networks. As distance and volume increase, the added fixed costs for voice-grade transmission via Data-Phone or equivalent (the Data-Phone equipment, the keyboarding and transmission equipment, and the receiving equipment or computer entry link) are offset by the savings on toll charges realized from the speed advantage which is increased 25 times. Data communications can also link a small company to a part-time computer (time shared or batch processing), allowing that company to use a computer easily when it cannot (or does not wish to) justify a full-time computer on its premises. Most important, the speed and convenience of data communications may justify its use when the intangible value of these advantages is estimated and entered into the balance.

COMPUTER PROGRAMMING

Stated in the simplest possible terms, computer programming is the activity of writing the "procedures manual" for the inanimate computer "operator" for each application put onto the computer. Each such "procedures manual" must be complete almost to the point of idiocy, since the most uncommon characteristic of the computer "operator" is common sense. If a computer is directed incorrectly by its program, Dr. Grace M. Hopper of Univac has observed, "it will compound the error infallibly and at incredible speed." The program must determine whether an input item makes sense to it (and if not, what to do with it), and then decide what processing path to follow for that item, based on its type. As described earlier, a program contains processing directions for each type of input item submitted for processing under its control. In processing any one item, only the portion of the program pertaining to that type of item is executed. (Most programming and computer operation difficulties arise from unanticipated item types.)

Current business computers users have experienced an initial programming cost that roughly equals the one-year cost of the hardware (rentals on the computer and associated equipment). This initial cost ratio does not decline appreciably over the first year or two because the using organization, as it learns to use its computer more effectively, improves or completely revises its programs in that period. The addition of applications for computer processing and the necessity of making changes to existing programs (to accommodate changed business goals or revised governmental regulations) combine to keep programming and programming costs in a computerized data processing system.

Fledgling computers users are beguiled by the availability from computer manufacturers of "standard" program packages for basic operations (e.g., sorting, statistical analysis, report generation) and even for complete applications such as charge account processing for department stores. The basic operation programs are indeed useful in simplifying applications programming (often at minor expense in computer processing time, insignificant in comparison with programming time and costs). The "standard" programs for complete applications, however, are seldom as standard as they are portrayed. To illustrate this, consider the case of a payroll processing service offered by a computer rental facility to over 300 small companies. Only 20 of these companies were willing or able to modify their payroll procedures to comply with the requirements of this standard processing procedure, despite the real savings the service offered them. Payroll processing is notoriously variable from company to company, yet its range of variation is probably not much greater than that in other common business applications as processed by different companies. Accordingly, "standard" applications programs usually require modifications, at the user's expense, to adapt them to his needs. Whether adaptable or not, these "standard" applications programs are excellent sources of suggestions for features to be included in similar programs.

The task of the computer programmer in preparing the "procedures manual" for an unimaginative (and untiring) "operator" is normally broken down into two phases: problem definition and reduction to detailed procedures, the latter usually called *coding*. Programming normally starts from broad problem definitions and general schemes for reduction to practice, which are developed by systems analysis (as discussed in succeeding chapters of this book). Given this start, the programmer defines the restricted problem assigned to him, with as much exactitude as possible. He then develops the fully detailed procedures to execute the operation for all acceptable variations of the input documents. The programmer's work interacts with systems analysis by raising questions that are best resolved at the higher level.

This relation between programming and systems analysis is worth exploring in more detail at this point. Take, as an example, a payroll processing application to be processed on a magnetic-tape-equipped computer (batch processing). Systems analysis will divide this application into a series of runs to be executed at different intervals; i.e., daily, weekly, monthly, annually. A daily run or group of runs is likely for editing of daily time cards (for completeness and self-consistency), conversion onto magnetic tape, sorting into master file order, and merging of each day's batch into a week-to-date file. If payroll is a weekly operation, there must be a weekly run or group of runs for payroll calculations (e.g., compute gross and net pay for each employee, print pay checks and a check ledger, do job cost analysis and overtime analysis, and print summary reports). Another weekly run is needed to correct the master file before the pay check run; these corrections include the addition of records for new employees, corrections to existing records to reflect changes in pay rate or number of deductions, etc. Finally, an annual run is needed to close out the payroll accounts and to prepare W-2 forms.

Having defined the runs for the entire application, systems analysis then develops the coordination needed to make them work together. In this example, the master file order and record layout must be defined at systems analysis level, since every run uses or is affected by the master file. In addition, systems analysis defines the forms used for submission of input and the reports to be issued by the whole system. Again, for this example, systems analysis determines the timecard forms and the summary report forms (where the latter are not determined by government regulation).

Systems analysis may turn over its definitions of each run in an application to a separate programmer; in any case, a programmer is concerned with only one run at a time, thus reducing the scope of his worries about an involved application. (For simpler applications, the programmer may perform much of what is described here as systems analysis.) The programmer now analyzes in exhaustive detail the problem area (the run) assigned to him, developing outlines of the execution procedures he will eventually code. These outlines and any unresolved questions are referred back to systems analysis for review and possible system changes. For example, the programmer doing the weekly pay check program may show an inordinate amount of processing for monthly commission payments to salesmen. Systems analysis can then determine whether to split off this part of the application into a separate monthly run. The programmer cannot decide this because he is unaware of its effect on the rest of the system. Yet it is the programmer's problem, brought to the attention of systems analysis, that causes a further refinement of the system. The interaction between systems analysis and programming is most common in decisions on *exception* handling, the handling of inputs that differ from the bulk type or types (like commission payments on a monthly basis in a weekly payroll operation). This subject of exception handling is discussed again in connection with systems analysis.

The programmer starts with the scope definition and coordination requirements set up by systems analysis, along with indications of the processing his program must provide to produce the desired outputs from the inputs supplied. The programmer's key tools during his problem definition phase are record layout diagrams and flow charts. Record layout diagrams show the size of each record type and the size and order of each *field* (discrete information item such as employee identification number) within the record. (See

EMPLOYEE NUMBER	EMPLOYEE NAME	STREET ADDRESS	TOWN	SOCIAL SECURITY NUMBER
1 8	9 34	35 52	53 70	71 80

GROSS PAY RATE	EXEMPT	HOSP INS	UNION D	OTHER D	QUARTER GROSS PAY TO DATE	QUARTER FICA PAY TO DATE	QUARTER FICA TAX TO DATE	YR-TO-DT GROSS	YR-TO-DT FEDERAL W'HOLD	YR-TO-DT STATE W'HOLD	YR-TO-DT OTHER W'HOLD
81 87	88	89	90	91	92 97	98 103	104 108	109 116	117 124	132	133 140

YR-TO-DT FICA GROSS	YR-TO-DT FICA TAX	DAYS WORKED	VAC DAYS ACCRUED	MEDICAL LEAVE	PERSONAL LEAVE
141 146	147 151	152 154	155 156	157 158	159 160

Figure 8. Record Layout Diagram

Figure 8.) If a record category includes different record types (e.g., weekly time records for piece-rate, hourly, and salaried employees), either a separate diagram is needed for each type, or if the fields do not vary with type, a tabulation of the types that are to be processed. For master file records, the order of these records is also needed; it is usually implied as the order of the item in the first information field (e.g., employee identification number). Systems analysis is likely to develop all these record layout diagrams for an involved application like payroll processing.

Flow charts provide a graphic description of the processing required for a complete application (both within and outside the computer) or, at a different level, a detailed outline of a single computer run or part of a run. The symbols used in flow charting to identify different processing operations and I/O media have varied in the past from user to user. However, a standard set of flow chart symbols has been adopted by the data processing industry. These symbols are shown in Figure 9. In both systems analysis and programming, two distinct levels of flow charting are normally used for problem definition: system flow charts (sometimes particularized as run diagrams at the programming level) and program or detailed flow charts (also called "block diagrams"). A system flow chart treats processing operations as "black boxes," stressing instead the inputs required and the outputs that result. At the programming level, a run diagram for a complete application shows the information flow through the entire processing sequence, detailing the division into runs for efficient computer use. This kind of diagram emphasizes the scheduling of runs, the procedures external to the computer, and the number of I/O devices needed for each run. As an example of a run diagram, Figure 10 shows the payroll processing application discussed previously. This diagram, or one like it, would be one of the products of systems analysis.

A program or detailed flow chart depicts the sequence and variety of processing steps within the processing box on a run diagram. This level of flow chart serves as the outline or block diagram of the program to be written for a particular run. If the program is likely to be a complex one, systems analysis may develop an over-all program flow chart to convey to the programmer what processing is required. The programmer then amplifies on this description by preparing more detailed program flow charts which show how he plans to write the program. By having these detailed program flow charts reviewed at the systems analysis level, the programmer confirms his understanding of the program to be written before he invests much time in coding, the next phase of his activity. His detailed flow charts also show whether he plans to write a straight-line program or to break the program into routines, each of which performs an isolable function. A straight-line program usually takes

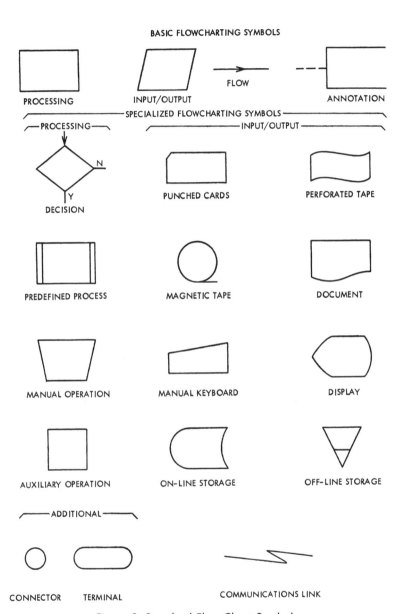

Figure 9. Standard Flow Chart Symbols

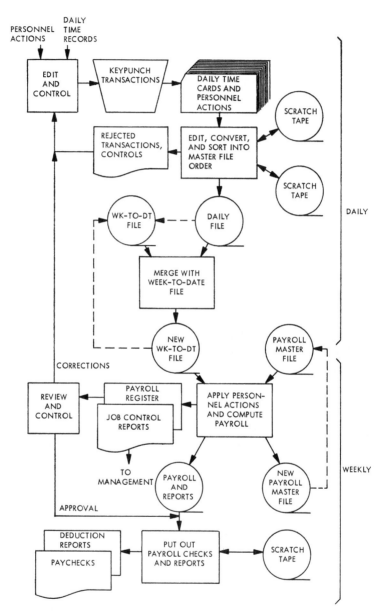

Figure 10. Typical Run Diagram

up less memory space and may run faster than a routinized program. However, a straight-line program is often more difficult to debug (i.e., make run correctly) and more difficult to change.

Both straight-line and routine approaches can employ preprogrammed segments (e.g., basic operation programs supplied by the computer manufacturer or previously written by the user organization). The choice between these two approaches, straight-line versus routine, may be based on the urgency for completion of the program or on the frequency of use or changes expected for the program. Figure 11 shows a detailed flow chart for a portion of the payroll processing application. Note the frequency of use of the decision box, the element of flexibility in computer processing.

After the problem definition phase of programming has been completed and checked out at the systems analysis level, the programmer must write or code the program; i.e., develop the sequence of instructions that the computer is to follow. A program can be written or coded in either of two forms:

1. Machine language (symbolic or absolute)
2. Problem-oriented language (e.g., COBOL, FORTRAN, PL/I, and others)

To write a program in absolute machine language, the programmer must state each instruction in the actual number or character pattern that the computer recognizes. In addition, he must assign an actual memory address for each instruction in the program and for each item of data within memory. A program so written can be transcribed onto a machine-readable medium (e.g., punched cards), loaded into the computer memory, and executed immediately. However, since the programmer must do all the bookkeeping (e.g., assigning addresses), writing a program in absolute machine language is a tedious and error-prone process. Furthermore, debugging an absolute program, particularly making extensive changes, is as difficult as writing the program from scratch.

Absolute programming was displaced early in the history of computer use by symbolic machine-language programming. Symbolic programming relieves the programmer of much bookkeeping

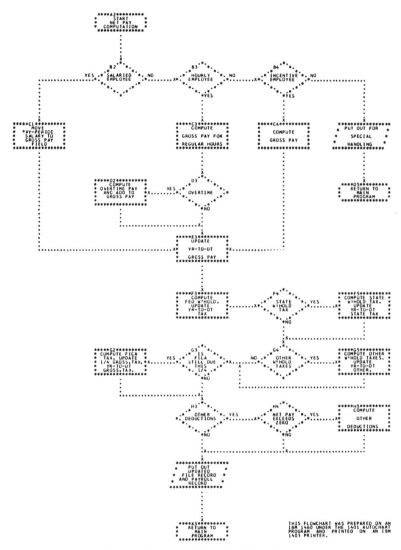

Figure 11. Typical Detailed Flow Chart

and difficult memorization. Each instruction in the computer repertory is assigned a *mnemonic* code, chosen for ease in remembering its meaning; e.g., the mnemonic code ADD is easier to remember than the equivalent in machine language, 110001. Some mnemonic codes are assigned for *pseudo-operations*, which are common programming steps such as defining a constant or reserving space in memory for input data. These pseudo-operations are not built into the computer but are performed by a preset series of computer instructions. In addition, some systems use *macro instruction* mnemonics to call preprogrammed segments from a library for incorporation into the processing program.

The most significant advance of symbolic over absolute programming is in the handling of address assignment. In symbolic programming, the programmer assigns *symbolic* or *relative* addresses to memory locations that his program must reference several times. The computer then converts these names for locations into absolute memory addresses. A symbolic address is simply an arbitrary name attached to an item of data or an instruction. A relative address locates the item at that address with respect to another item. For example, if the first instruction in a routine is addressed symbolically as START, the next instruction can be addressed relatively as START + 1. A programmer writing a symbolic program need specify only one absolute address, the location at which his program is to start. The computer assigns addresses consecutively from that starting location. In the process, it converts each symbolic and relative address into its absolute equivalent, freeing the programmer of that task.

A symbolic program cannot be executed immediately upon submission to the computer, since it must be *assembled;* i.e., converted by the computer under control of an assembler program into an absolute machine-language program. The assembler program interprets each mnemonic code as follows:

1. If the mnemonic is for a computer instruction, the machine-language equivalent is substituted.
2. If the mnemonic specifies a pseudo-operation, the assembler program executes it.

3. If the mnemonic specifies a macro instruction, the assembler program incorporates the appropriate preprogrammed segment from the library into the machine-language program.

The assembler program also assigns absolute addresses and checks for programmer errors. This error checking is limited to detection of rule violations, principally incorrect assembly or symbolic language statements, not detection of errors in processing logic. If the assembly process is completed, with no serious errors found in the coding, the assembled machine-language program can then be executed by the computer. The assembly time costs of symbolic programming are more than offset by the savings in programming time. In fact, absolute machine-language programming is seldom used except for "patching" (inserting short, corrective steps) in assembled programs or for special programs that are critical insofar as memory space or execution time is concerned.

Although symbolic programming relieves the programmer of many time-consuming tasks, it still ties the programmer to a specific computer; i.e., it is machine-oriented. In fact, machine-language instructions can be included directly in a symbolic program. The programmer must know a computer quite well to write a symbolic program for it. Further, a symbolic program written for one computer cannot easily be shifted to another computer for assembly and execution. To answer these objections, several problem-oriented programming languages have been developed. Best known of these are COBOL (Common Business Oriented Language), FORTRAN (Formula Translator), and IBM's PL/I (formerly NPL, or New Programming Language).

COBOL was developed expressly to reduce the training needed by programmers and to allow program interchange between different computers. A COBOL programming manual contains a large set of pattern statements in "ruly" English (these rules make machine translation possible). A programmer simply modifies these pattern statements and arranges them in the sequence necessary to describe the procedures of his program. (A Japanese version of COBOL uses English pattern sentences; the explanations are in Japanese, however.) A program written in COBOL is submitted to a computer for translation from this *source* program form into *object* program (i.e., machine language) form under control of that computer's *compiler* program. If the processing program is to be run on a different computer, the *source* program is submitted for compiling on that computer, with little or no reprogramming.

A COBOL program contains four divisions, as follows:

1. Identification division, differentiating this program from any others
2. Environment division, specifying the computer and I/O devices on which the source program is to be compiled and, if different, the computer and I/O devices on which the object program is to be executed
3. Data division, describing the input, output, and file record formats
4. Procedure division, stating the processing steps in "ruly" English

Of these four divisions, only the environment division is tied directly to a computer (or computers), but the data division may also be affected by changes in available I/O devices. However, any reprogramming that may be required to switch execution to a different computer is greatly simplified by this segregation of affected elements in the program. The versatility implied by allowing compilation on one computer for execution on another is limited in practice by the availability of "mixed" compilers. Generally, a COBOL program can be compiled on a computer with a large memory, for execution on the same type of computer having a smaller memory because compilation may be impossible with the smaller memory.

FORTRAN differs from COBOL in that it is designed more for science-engineering processing than for business processing. Mathematical statements in a science or engineering program are stated almost unchanged in FORTRAN. (FORTRAN is sometimes called procedure-oriented because of this feature.) However, it is somewhat improper to speak of a single FORTRAN, since it was not developed for interchangeability between computers (standardization efforts began in 1962, with only tentative results by 1966). Instead, different computers have been provided with different FORTRAN *compilers,* each usually offering slightly different features closely matched to the computer. As a result, a FORTRAN source program written to meet the rules of one compiler cannot in general be compiled successfully on a different computer.

IBM's PL/I (originally called NPL) includes both COBOL and the features of FORTRAN in its structure, with improvements in both areas and with other advanced features. For example, the COBOL subset of PL/I includes an improved report generator and direct conversion between dollars and pounds sterling. The advantages and improvements of PL/I are somewhat undercut by the compatible features of the computer line for which IBM is implementing PL/I (a reservation valid for all problem-oriented languages, as discussed below). As of early 1966, only one other computer manufacturer has agreed to implement PL/I (by providing compilers), but others are likely to follow in the face of competitive pressure.

Probably the most telling argument in favor of problem-oriented languages is that programmers need less training before they begin to produce useful programs. COBOL, with its "ruly" English, is relatively easy to learn, although it is exacting to use. (As one programmer describes it, "You can be sloppy as you like in the procedure division, but you have to describe the world down to the last atom in the other three divisions.") Similarly, FORTRAN allows engineers to state their procedures in almost unchanged mathematical form. Machine languages (whether absolute or symbolic) are neither English nor mathematics and so require more effort to learn. Another argument in favor of problem-oriented languages is that they automatically generate adequate program documentation; i.e., someone other than the programmer can easily follow and understand what the program is doing. Documentation can be a serious problem in machine-oriented programming because it depends on the programmer's addition of comments to his coding and his maintenance of flow charts in comprehensible and up-to-date form. Documentation is important for systems integration, as a guard against personnel turnover, and for ease in making changes to a program. However, problem-oriented languages do not necessarily solve the problem. More than one programming manager has commented, wonderingly, on a programmer who could write efficient, yet incomprehensible, programs in the "ruly" English of COBOL.

The protection of programs (and programmers) from obsolescence when a new computer is brought onto the scene is no longer a significant advantage of problem-oriented languages since the introduction of compatible lines of computers (as discussed in the previous chapter). Even the interchangeability of programs in problem-oriented languages between computers is a less significant feature, since an object program for one model in a compatible line can be executed on any other model with equivalent memory size and I/O devices. (This interchangeability is important in handling overloads and when a computer is down for maintenance.)

There are some drawbacks in the use of problem-oriented programming languages. First, in compiling a source program, more computer time is required than for assembly of an equivalent symbolic program. (This added machine time may be compensated for by the reduction in programming time, particularly for single-run or "one-shot" programs.) Along the same line, a change to a source program usually requires a complete recompiling, whereas a machine-language programmer can normally write a "patch" in absolute language to handle a small change, thus avoiding the expense of reassembly. Second, the goal of interchangeability between computers tends to reduce the capabilities of a problem-oriented language to the lowest common denominator among computers, ignoring the unique features of a particular computer. It is true that the compiler for a specific computer is theoretically designed to make full use of all its features. Yet the computer user who has only problem-oriented language knowledge is in no position to evaluate the effectiveness of the compiler he is using (or the efficiency of the object language it produces). Third, the divorce of programming from machine design considerations can easily lead to careless programming. For example, if a program requires the calculation of the expression

$$ax^2 + bx + c,$$

it can be written just that way in a problem-oriented language. The COBOL or FORTRAN statement would read

$$\mathsf{RESULT = A*X**2 + B*X + C}$$

where * means "times," or multiply, and ** means "raised to the power of."

A machine-language programmer will remember that a multiplication step takes much time (three to twelve times more than the time for an addition step). He will also notice that the expression can be rewritten to eliminate one multiplication, as follows:

$$x(ax + b) + c$$

or, in the notation of COBOL or Fortran,

$$\mathsf{X*(A*X + B) + C}$$

The resultant saving in computer execution time may never occur to a problem-oriented language programmer. It is questionable, however, whether savings of this sort justify the costs of added training and care in programming that are required to realize them.

A similar question of the balance between programming costs and computer execution time (translatable into cost figures) arises with computers that offer both *fixed point* binary and *floating point* binary arithmetic instructions (as do the compatible computer lines, although floating point binary arithmetic is an extra-cost option in most lines). Fixed point binary arithmetic ignores the position of the binary point in a binary word. (The binary point is equivalent to the decimal point, separating the whole and fractional parts of the number.) In fixed point arithmetic, the programmer must keep track of the binary point; for example, he must align the binary points of two numbers before he has them added. Floating point arithmetic splits each word into two parts, an *exponent* that locates the binary point and a *fraction* that expresses the significant figures in the word. An equivalent procedure with decimal numbers would express 3,425.721 as 0.3425721 $\times$ 10^4, and then write it as exponent 4 and fraction 3425721. Floating point arithmetic relieves the programmer of accounting for the position of the binary point, but its operations take more time than do fixed point operations. If a program is to be executed only once or twice, the choice is clearly in favor of floating point arithmetic, to save programming time. However, if the program is to be run many times, the added programming costs to prepare a fixed point arithmetic program may be recovered many times over.

Similarly, the choice between machine-language programming and problem-oriented language programming is dependent upon the balance between programming time and the total time devoted to program execution, modified somewhat by the expected frequency of changes to the program in question. A one-shot program is clearly better done in a problem-oriented language to minimize programming time (unless the programmer can pick up preprogrammed segments in machine-language form from other sources, an advantage that can be capitalized on in routinized programming). Conversely, a program that is to be executed often and without changes is likely to be more efficient if it is written in machine language. The added cost in programming time will be recovered many times over from the savings in efficient execution. (One very conservative estimate equates 1 hour of machine compilation or assembly time to 4 hours of programming time. The ratio of programming time to execution time is much higher, regardless of the programming language. A program that takes weeks to write may be executed in minutes, if not in seconds.)

The appearance of compatible computers has shifted the advantage to machine-language programming for all but one-shot (or nearly so) programs. Yet both machine-language and problem-oriented language programming are likely to survive and prosper, since the premise for choice between them is probably a false one. The compatible computer lines were developed only after the computer designers recognized the distinction between their hardware problems and the logical problems of those who used computers.

That distinction made it possible for the designers to produce computers that could handle any and all applications. In the same way, a programmer who recognizes the distinction between short-run changeable programs and long-run relatively invariant programs can best choose the language in which to write these programs. After all, complete ignorance of the computer exercised by a program is as wasteful for a programmer as is encyclopedic knowledge of computer inner workings.

DATA PROCESSING ADMINISTRATION

The administration of a data processing system encompasses the scheduling of, and the follow-through on, all activities within the system, to assure that it meets its goals. This administration is distinct from that of the applications handled by the system; for example, the company controller still administers the general accounting function within his company, even after its detailed handling is transferred onto a computer. Data processing administration directs the processing system as a tool for other administrative groups within the company, achieving the greatest possible efficiency in serving their needs.

Whether a data processing system is large or small, whether it uses an on-premises computer or a part-time computer off premises, the system elements to be administered are the same:

1. The computer and its operating staff
2. The input data conversion personnel (key punchers, verifiers, supervisor, etc.)
3. The systems analysts and the programmers

These elements are described in terms of personnel, since it is in this relation that their applications are usually coordinated. With a fully staffed data processing operation on premises, all three elements are employed within the using organization. At the other extreme, time-shared or batch processing on an off-premises computer, the using organization may staff only the second functional group, yet it must deal with off-premises personnel who provide the other two functions. Effective administration is vital for either extreme as well as for all intermediate cases.

Because a data processing system is (or should be) a tool for use by all administrative groups within a company, its administrator must have access to a high enough level in the company to avoid being committed, uneconomically, to only one of the company's administrative groups. Decisions on data processing (particularly, resolution of conflicting demands) must be referable to the top management level in the company, which is, incidentally, the level that stands to gain most from this tool. As will be seen later in this book, reporting at this top level is imperative during the initial study and system design phases if the best computerized data processing system is to be developed. Nor does the importance of reporting at this top level diminish after a system is installed.

In a large data processing system, the internal administrative function is carried by the computer operators' supervisor, the key punching supervisor, and the analyst programmer supervisor, all reporting to the data processing manager. Demand processing and data communications may eliminate (or reduce) the need for key punching (and its supervisor) as well as downgrading the need for an operators' supervisor on the grounds that the computer operator has less to do in a demand processing system. As system size decreases, systems analysis is reduced to the initial effort only and programming is curtailed to the handling of short-term or small changes to programs (better described as program maintenance). In fact, a combination programmer-computer operator can be assigned for first-shift operation of a small computer installation if it is on a demand processing basis. Since the computer is unaware of working overtime, although its manufacturer may require additional rental payments to cover the extra maintenance costs arising from the added use of the computer's units, most computer users keep their machines on a two-shift or even three-shift schedule. A programmer assigned as first-shift operator is on the company's premises while the users he may need to consult are there as well. Second- and third-shift operators have little other than the computer to talk to, if they wish to talk at all. However, it is not worthwhile to employ a programmer as a computer operator, whatever the shift, unless he is allowed time to do programming between the demands on him for computer operation. For this reason, demand processing, with its relaxation of requirements on the computer operator, is essential if a programmer is to serve as computer operator and perform useful programming as well.

When a computerized data processing system uses an off-premises computer (time shared or in batch processing), the needed personnel loading drops down to the requirements imposed by data conversion. Computer operation personnel are provided by the computer center. Systems analysts and programmers may be provided by the same source or by another supplier. In these circumstances, the administrative loading also drops, yet the need to report to the company's top level does not diminish. A company using this approach to computerized data processing can best serve its needs by assigning the administration of data processing to a top-level executive who understands the field but does not devote full time to it. As indicated earlier, most of the in-house work for data processing in this kind of system is data conversion; this work can be supervised by a key punching (or equivalent) supervisor who reports to the top-level executive. That executive must also be able to deal with computer-operator supervisors, systems analysts, programmers, and their managers. The task, even as a secondary assignment, is not negligible. Hopefully, this book will supply the knowledge required by an executive with the acumen necessary to handle this kind of task.

4

WHAT ARE THE GOALS
OF A COMPUTERIZED BUSINESS
DATA PROCESSING SYSTEM?

This survey of the role and capabilities of the computer in a business data processing system would be incomplete if there were no discussion of the goals to be achieved by the computer system. Accordingly, this chapter examines these goals, and in addition lays out the pattern of the procedures for evaluating and implementing them. Although these procedures are covered in detail in the remainder of this book, the treatment in this chapter serves to introduce the succeeding text and to show the relations that may be obscured by the normal topical divisions of the book.

COMPUTER SYSTEM GOALS

Two phrases descriptive of computer systems for business data processing are currently in the air; they are the *total system* concept and the *management information system*. The total system idea calls for the handling of all data processing within a company by its computer. A management information system is one that provides, on demand from management, up-to-the-minute reports on any and all aspects of company operation. Both concepts are worth serious consideration as goals for a computer system. However, for small systems, the total system concept is better treated as an ideal than as a concrete goal. The cost of performing low-volume applications on a computer can far exceed the cost of performing them manually at nearly the same speed.

As an extreme example of a low-volume application, consider the task of preparing the pay check for a company president. Probably, that task is now done by the company treasurer, who spends perhaps 5 minutes each pay period on it. Even at the treasurer's salary, the task is done more cheaply than it might be on a computer, with far fewer people privy to the president's pay scale. Computer processing of executive (i.e., president and just below) payroll is usually justified only in very large organizations, and then more for consistency than for speed or economy in processing. Ultimately, the total system concept as a computer system goal is subordinate to the profitability goal. As will be seen, it is often absorbed by other goals.

The idea of a management information system as a computer system goal is a valuable one if it is considered as an integral aspect of the computer system. Ideally, management should be able to request, and receive in short order, a timely report on any part of its company operations. Yet, a well-designed computer system reduces the need for spot reports almost to the vanishing point; it is designed to provide management with just the information needed precisely as the need arises. Along with its routine handling of routine operations, the system extracts and digests information for concise presentation to management. The presentation is either a summary report for over-all surveillance or a "flag" report that requests prompt management attention and decision. In essence, a well-designed computer system for business data processing is a management information system, a tool designed expressly to support management in the efficient direction of the company.

When the design of a computer system emphasizes its role as a management tool, it makes use of the total system idea in two ways. First, within the limits of cost justification, the computer system combines naturally related functions that are performed separately in manual processing, thus approaching a total system horizontally. Second, the design of a computer system requires redefinition of the goals to be met by the function and, usually, a reassignment of tasks for more efficient operation. The computer can take over routine decision making (e.g., reordering of low-inventory stock items, with lead time allowed for delivery), leaving only nonroutine matters to be passed on to management. This technique, called *management by exception*, enhances the computer system value as a management tool by allowing management to concentrate on nontrivial operating problems of the company. The reassessment and reassignment of tasks within the function to be converted for computer processing implies a vertical approach to a total system for that function. In both aspects of computer system design, the application of computer "logic," more than computer speed, to business data processing is what yields returns.

A simple illustration of the redefinition process is possible in connection with the processing of credit accounts (e.g., in department stores, parts distributors). In manual processing, transactions (charges and payments) may be posted only in journals for final processing at the end of each month. In final processing, the transactions are applied to update each account, the account is aged (previous month's amount due becomes the amount due for sixty days, and so on), and decisions are made to stop further credit to delinquent accounts. In addition, of course, monthly invoices are prepared and mailed. If this function is to serve as a more efficient management tool when converted for computer processing, the daily transactions should be applied daily against their accounts, developing a daily report of delinquent or overextended accounts so that further credit to them can be stopped. Better still, if the function is performed on a demand or on-line system, each new order is checked for its effect on the account's credit limit on a current basis. If the limit is exceeded, the new order is blocked by the computer; a management decision is needed to override the block and extend credit beyond the account limit. In this demand processing approach, management is not bothered about delinquent accounts (except in periodic summary reports) unless these accounts try to exceed their credit limit; this is truly management by exception.

The ultimate goal of a computer system for business data processing is profitability. Unfortunately, except in special cases, the computer contribution to profits may not be easily identified, whereas its contribution to company costs is all too obvious. What portion of company profits can be attributed to the elimination of clerical errors by the computer or to improvements in management control? Can you assess the savings accountable from inventory reduction and faster order handling made possible by a computer? What is the value of increased customer acceptance of company service (e.g., allowing bank depositors to deal with any bank branch by providing demand processing at a central location which services all branches)? It is true that a computer may offer a lower operating cost than the clerical staff it replaces in a particular function. However, these savings over clerical costs can be wiped out by the costs outside the computer itself (e.g., data conversion facilities and personnel, program maintenance), to say nothing of the initial costs of programming and of conversion to the computer system. These initial costs must be written off over the first two or more years of computer system operation if a realistic picture of system costs is to be developed. As noted above, all these cost elements are readily apparent. The logical question that follows from this discussion is, "How can conversion to computer data processing be justified, with assurance of profitability within a reasonable interval?"

Large companies have been able to justify conversion to a computer system by showing that its costs for performance of one function within the company were comparable to current costs for that function and that the computer system had surplus capacity to handle other separate functions at little or no additional cost. "Comparable" costs varied from 80 to 150 per cent of current costs, including apportionment of initial costs over at least two years. In smaller companies, no single function may show a cost comparable to that for a computer system, yet the basic principle is the same; if necessary, two or more functions and their costs can be analyzed for approximate parity with the cost of a computer system that offers additional capacity for other functions. If a realistic (or better, pessimistic) appraisal of computer system costs approaches current system costs for the same functions, the well-designed computer system is justified. Of course, as computer prices decline, this multiple function justification becomes less important, even for small companies.

Questions appropriate at this point include, "What about the costs of finding out whether a computer system can be justified? Aren't these costs an important element of initial cost when conversion follows? How are they justified when the decision goes against use of a computer?" Surprisingly, perhaps, the companies that have gone through the process of justifying (or rejecting) use of a computer, usually called a *feasibility study*, have recovered its costs in less than a year from savings revealed by the study. These savings came from the application of computer "logic" to current operations, leading to the elimination of duplicate procedures, consolidation of separate operations, and other consequences of reconsidering company goals within the study area. In view of this experience, the costs of a feasibility study need not be justified if a negative decision is the result, nor need they be included in initial conversion costs of a computer system. If anything, a feasibility study is profitable in and of itself, if its discoveries are put to use.

THE ROAD TO COMPUTER USAGE

A feasibility study is only the first phase of a three-phase process for conversion from manual to computerized data processing. The three phases are:

1. The feasibility study
2. System design
3. System conversion and installation

The process is considered in three phases both for convenience in presentation and because the phases offer economical breakpoints, logical points for a decision to proceed or to stop. The feasibility study concludes when the decision is made to convert or not to convert. If the process continues into the system design phase, the system goals and constraints established during feasibility study define the system design effort to implement them most efficiently. System design develops the features of a computer system that meets, at acceptable cost, the functional goals set for it. The system design phase is essentially finished when a specific computer and associated equipment are chosen for the system. Thereafter, unless system design is ended by a decision not to use a computer, all activities fall into the system conversion and installation phase. This phase particularizes the system design for the selected computer, converts company files and procedures for computer processing, staffs and trains operating personnel, and installs and transfers operation onto the computer.

This division of the conversion process is artificial in some respects. Both the feasibility study and the system design phases involve systems analysis. They are intimately related, since the feasibility study provides the base from which system design starts. Similarly, system conversion and installation carries forward the results of system design. Finally, all three phases are ultimately the responsibility of company management at top level, even when the three phases are each executed by a different group (e.g., management consultants, computer manufacturer sales support groups, contract systems analysts). The division into phases is, however, convenient for scheduling of the whole process and, of course, for budgeting its costs. Yet the continuity of the process must not be ignored, regardless of its necessary division into phases in the remainder of this book.

PART II

THE FEASIBILITY STUDY

A feasibility study allows management to determine whether all or part of the data processing within the company can be converted profitably onto a computer, with reasonable assurance that the study costs will be recouped even if the computer is rejected. Working within a predefined functional area of company operations, the feasibility study first establishes in detail the procedures used presently and the volume of data handled. Next it determines the cost and efficiency of these procedures and forces a redefinition of the goals met (or not met) by current operations. Finally, the study develops a broad plan for computer processing in the area being analyzed, as a basis for estimates of computer system costs and benefits for that application. With all this information in hand, management can reach an informed decision on the use of a computer.

At first sight, a feasibility study appears to be no more than a methods and procedures analysis of the area under study; in fact, this aspect of the study yields most of its returns. A feasibility study goes beyond methods and procedures analysis, however, by analyzing the whole application in the light of computer capabilities. The techniques of methods and procedures analysis are used, but have a different aim.

The question often raised at this point is, "Why analyze current operation if it's going to be changed?" The first answer is that current operation may not be changed, either because a computer is too expensive for the application or because current operation embodies the best procedures for the application. Without this complete analysis, some unique capabilities of the current system may be omitted from a new processing system, to its detriment. Second, unless the procedures, volume, costs, and goals of the current system are evaluated in detail, no valid estimate of costs for an optimum computer system is possible, and no valid comparison can be made for a decision on continuation to system design. Finally, a system designer can best learn the application and its requirements by performing a thorough analysis of the current system. Further, his participation with top management in its re-evaluation of system goals demonstrates and confirms his understanding of company objectives within the study area.

Another question usually arises as to the personnel who will perform the feasibliity study. In a large company, a team of systems analysts is assigned for months or even years to a feasibility study, after the company planning board has selected the area to be studied and has received management approval for the study. In a small company, the effort may be correspondingly smaller; a company executive may perform a preliminary study, often without leaving his desk, by collecting the information described in Chapter 5. However, a feasibility study is best performed in detail by someone who is both trained in systems analysis and familiar with computer system capabilities. Most executives have neither the time nor the inclination to obtain this training, and so either hire a specialist or call in outside services. Yet they must know enough about the specialty to make best use of its practitioners. To acquaint them with these principles is the goal of subsequent chapters.

One final question may remain: "What about calling on a computer manufacturer to perform the feasibility study?" The answer is that it is unfair to both the computer manufacturer and the prospective computer user. If the problem and its requirements cannot be stated in any detail, the computer salesman cannot give an accurate recommendation, and the prospective user cannot evaluate the recommendation adequately. Computer manufacturers find that their unhappy installations are those that were proposed by overoptimistic salesmen on the basis of inadequate information and accepted by uncritical customers. Their sales support staffs can offer much valuable advice and assistance to prospective computer users (particularly in the system design phase), but their aid is more useful after the user has completed most of his feasibility study. At that stage, the prospective user better understands his needs for a computer and can better use the support of computer manufacturers. Before that stage is reached, the computer manufacturers can provide only generalized suggestions and orientation for the uses of their products.

5

THE PATTERN OF
A FEASIBILITY STUDY

The details of a feasibility study vary to match the company and the application being studied, but a general pattern holds true under the level of these detailed differences. This pattern starts with the gathering of information on current procedures and data volumes. Forms used in the current operation are collected and annotated, descriptions of the files used are compiled, and the detailed procedures are determined, usually by interviewing operating personnel. This collected information is then analyzed and codified, normally on flow charts that also carry the volume and flow rate of data being processed at each step or station in the current system. The accuracy of this codification is verified by auditing the procedures it depicts before this phase of the study is completed. Finally, these results are reviewed with management, stressing possible revisions of restraints, organization, and goals of the processing system, to allow more efficient achievement of company objectives.

Most of this chapter is devoted to a description of this pattern for a feasibility study, and presents the techniques and approaches that have been developed with experience in studies of this kind. This chapter begins, however, with a discussion of the ground rules that are necessary for a successful study.

GROUND RULES FOR A FEASIBILITY STUDY

A feasibility study normally starts in response to a problem in current operations. The problem may be a real one, identified by failure of the current system to meet its schedules, or by increased overtime, or by work backlogs in a particular area. Equally likely, the problem may be a virtual one (either potential or imagined), raised by glowing descriptions of a new computer by its manufacturer, or by reports that a competitor has installed a computer (or other data processing equipment) and is about to reap immense benefits from its use. Whatever the problem, it will not be understood clearly unless a feasibility study is undertaken. The study resolves the ill-defined case of a virtual problem; it also avoids the narrow solution of a specific, real problem.

The study may be proposed by one group within the company, even at a relatively low level within that group. If administration of the study is left at that level or within that group, most of its advantages will be forfeited. Like the computer system it may lead to, the study must be performed for, and with the active support of, top management within the company. The study must have access to the entire area designated for analysis, an area that will cut across current organizational lines if the study is to be of maximum value. After all, one potential benefit of the study stems from the consolidation of currently separate operations. To evaluate this potential, the study must be free to investigate all these separate operations, a freedom possible only with the support of top management. In addition, a study administered by one organizational element is restricted to the limited goals of that element. Finally, since the feasibility study raises questions about company objectives and the means to achieve them, the study must have access to the management levels at which these questions can be resolved. The ultimate decision to which the study leads, "to computerize or not to computerize" (with apologies to Will Shakespeare), can be answered only by top management.

The study scope and its schedule should also be established before the major study effort starts, to prevent diffuse and wasteful activities. The scope sets out the principal area to be analyzed, allowing continuation into naturally related areas (upon approval from management) while precluding vague expenditures of time and money. Since a company contains more than one possible study area, a choice is necessary. Usually, the choice includes the problem area that motivated the study, but is not confined exclusively to that area. More valuable results come from a study that encompasses a fairly large functional area within the company (e.g., sales order processing or some other, more appropriate grouping of conventional processing operations on a functional basis). If no problem triggered the study, the choice should be the functional area that can most benefit from computer processing; i.e., that area with highest costs for current processing or that with highest volume of data being processed in a disciplined way, or both areas. If the computer can be justified for the chosen area, it can later accept other, less justifiable areas to provide a greater return on computer system investment without significantly increasing computer system costs. The opposite approach of considering an area that benefits only slightly from computer processing may wrongly preclude adoption of a computer system because it is found that its costs are too high for this low-benefit area.

The scope of the study cannot be defined precisely without some preliminary survey of the areas that might be studied. Similarly, the study schedule cannot be drawn up until the scope of the study is defined and some basis for a time estimate is available. Both elements for schedule determination are developed during the preliminary survey, to be described. The study schedule should allow enough time for a thorough investigation, yet force concentration on the defined study area. A schedule extension is justified if, with management approval, the scope of the study is extended. Otherwise, the schedule should be observed fairly closely, if only to avoid the effects of the "law of diminishing returns."

PRELIMINARY SURVEY

The preliminary survey to establish the scope and schedule for a feasibility study is an informal procedure. It has been described as a broad-brush treatment of the formal study, ascertaining where in the company a computer system might be useful. The survey can be conducted by requesting reports from operating supervisors in the areas under consideration. These reports, all describing volumes on the same time interval (e.g., a week or a month), should contain the following information:

1. The sources of input documents and the destinations of output documents.
2. The volume of each type of document processed.
3. The time at which input documents arrive (e.g., at every mail delivery, at the start of the business day, or Friday at 5 o'clock), and the maximum, minimum, and average quantity of documents in any one batch.
4. The average time to process an average document; this is equivalent to the number of documents processed per day by one person, not to the results of a time and motion study.
5. Any schedule requirements on the processing operation (e.g., pay checks must be issued within three working days after the close of the pay period).
6. The labor loading, including supervisory, for the operation; this can be given as the total regular and overtime hours by job category over the processing period; equivalently, it can be the number of people, including part-time workers, engaged in the operation plus the average amount of overtime worked.
7. The cost of equipment used, ranging from desks and files on up through business equipment such as desk calculators, and the floor space occupied by the operation.

Items 1 through 5 should be available from each supervisor with little effort; items 6 and 7 may better come from other sources such as the payroll department and the purchasing department or office manager.

The information from these reports will not be detailed enough (nor, possibly, accurate enough) for a full feasibility study. It should, however, provide an over-all picture of the company data processing operations within the area selected for possible study. A flow chart can be prepared from these reports to show the interactions between separate processing operations, as well as the volume of data through each operation. This depiction usually shows obvious boundaries for the feasibility study, clearly associating those operations that are related and distinguishing those that interact only negligibly with the rest of the system. The survey may thus lead to a scope definition for the feasibility study that was not anticipated before the preliminary survey was undertaken; indeed, the relations discovered by the survey may have no explicit counterparts in the formal company organization.

The cost figures for current operations are useful in at least two ways. First, these figures set a bound on the budget for the feasibility study, which is effectively a limit on its scope. A study budgeted for more than a year's worth of processing costs seems unreasonable, even if the budget is likely to be recovered in short order. There is no hard-and-fast rule governing the ratio of current processing costs to the costs of a reasonable feasibility study. Yet, it is worth noting that a company allots more time and funds for its second study than for its first, expecting thus to avoid the costly errors stemming from the first (and presumably inadequate) study. Of equal importance, current cost figures determine in a rough way the size of the computer system that the study can justify, barring a drastic change in management objectives. The costs of a proposed computer system are ultimately compared with these current costs, thus limiting the system to a large or a small computer (or a part-time computer if that is available) on the basis of these costs. This limit is important to the feasibility study, since it determines the emphasis of the study, whether on a computer of whatever size, on a part-time computer, or on other data processing equipment of less-than-computer capability (e.g., typewriter-calculators). The feasibility study is less affected by this limit than is the system design phase. Nonetheless, it is valuable in helping to determine early the ball park in which the game is to be played.

The preliminary survey, as described so far, can establish the scope of a feasibility study but not its schedule, apart from the budgetary limits based on current processing costs. A time estimate for the study is based on information needed for the study. This information can be collected during the preliminary survey and submitted to the systems analyst so that he can produce the time estimate on which the schedule is based. Alternatively, the analyst may be allowed time (e.g., a week) for this preliminary phase of his study, to gather the initial information he needs for an adequate time estimate. The information needed for this phase of his study includes:

1. Any and all documentation of current procedures within the area under study, modified by evaluation of the accuracy and currency of this documentation; the more complete and up-to-date this documentation is, the shorter the formal study can be.

2. A collation of all forms, records, and reports that are originated by, entered into, or used within the area under study; these documents should be annotated, as described in succeeding portions of this chapter, but this annotation may be left for execution by the analyst in the course of the study.

3. The organizational structure within the study area, both in its formal presentation and as it actually operates (quite different aspects, usually, of the "same" structure).

The need for this array of information may not be apparent at this point. Yet, as simple a step as the collation of all forms used within the study area can be an informative one; managers who have tried it have been surprised to find 200 forms where they expected only 50. A feasibility study goes well beyond this array in its investigation of the area under examination; this array serves as an indication of the complexity of its task.

STUDY METHODS AND MOTIVES

A feasibility study is concerned primarily with documentation in complete detail of the procedures of the current processing operations, of the volume by type of procedure, and of the facilities (e.g., files) needed for each procedure. The first and last of these elements will have direct counterparts in any computer data processing system that replaces the current one; the information on volume by type of procedure is a measure of the complexity needed in the computer system. Secondarily, the feasibility study examines the efficiency of current organization and procedures in view of computer capabilities and presents this examination for management review and approval. Finally, the feasibility study produces a broad plan for a computer system, which embodies all the necessary features of the current system, all the general improvements submitted to and approved by management (after consideration of their likely cost), and reasonable provision for growth in both this application and others that may be added to the computer system.

At this stage, since the plan for the computer system includes detailed information on procedures, data volumes, and processing schedules (including the growth factor predicted for the useful life of the computer system), management can either continue the feasibility study to obtain recommendations from the systems analyst or call in several computer manufacturers to request their suggestions and informal cost estimates on the equipment needed to implement the planned system. This end phase is treated in more detail in the next chapter; its presentation here indicates the goal of the procedures to be described.

As just stated, the feasibility study must gather information on current procedures, volume by type of procedure, and necessary facilities for these procedures. This information-gathering phase is simplified considerably if current procedures in the area under study are documented adequately; the documentation is adequate if it is complete and up to date. If not, procedural information must be gathered by the systems analyst in interviews with operating personnel, unfortunately to the occasional detriment of current operations. These interviews may also be necessary, but of shorter duration, to verify the accuracy of procedural documentation, whatever its source. When no documentation exists and the interview technique seems too disruptive or too expensive, an alternate technique for information gathering can be used, although its results are less satisfactory than those of the interview method. This alternate technique, essentially an extension of the one used in the preliminary survey, requests detailed descriptions of procedures from selected operating personnel and from their supervisors, prepared by them at their own convenience. The responses to these requests will vary in completeness unless they are guided by questionnaires as detailed as the interviews they replace.

Information about volume by type of procedure is needed in the study as a gauge of the complexity of the computer system to be proposed in place of the current system. Remember that a computer is *par excellence* an executor of routine operations. The efficiency of a batch processing computer goes up as the volume of similar items increases and as the length of the run on a single category of items increases. This run length decreases as the variety of items to be processed by the run is increased, since the program must be enlarged to deal with each type in that category of input items. The efficiency of demand processing is even more dependent on limiting the variety of items to be processed (with much less importance accorded to the volume of any one type of input data).

A demand processor requires a different program for each type of input data to be processed, thereby needing more random access storage for each additional program (and type of input data). A demand processor must also spend some time on each input item to determine its type; i.e., the program appropriate for its processing. This type determination time, which is not directly useful processing time, increases with the number of different types of input items to be processed. Thus, the complexity of the computer system to replace current procedures or, equivalently, its efficiency depends on the volume-by-type (sometimes called *frequency distribution*) information gathered during the feasibility study.

Volume-by-type information is not particularly useful (except on an over-all basis) unless it is supplemented by information about data flow rates and schedule requirements. The latter are particularly important for a potential batch processing operation; both are necessary if demand processing is contemplated for the area under study. In either kind of processing, data flow rates describe the maximum, average, and minimum data volume of a particular type within a unit-time interval. For demand processing, this unit-time interval may be as long as an hour or, for high-volume applications, as short as 1 second. For batch processing, data flow rates are more meaningfully stated in terms of batch size (again maximum, average, and minimum) and interval between batch arrivals. Maximum data flow rate (or, equivalently, maximum batch size) imposes the severest requirements on the system; a design that accommodates only the average load, while cheaper, may be falsely economical. The latter situation recalls the bridge designer who dutifully surveyed the mast heights of all vessels that traversed the waterway his bridge was to cross and then designed his bridge to clear those vessels with average mast height or lower, thereby barring the passage of all larger vessels. In general, a computer system can be designed to accommodate all but unusual peak loads without jeopardizing its feasibility; the surplus capacity available in off-peak periods can be readily applied to less urgent applications, with consequent advantages for the using organization.

The schedule requirements of an operation are critical for batch processing; they are equally applicable to operations that are to be batched on a time-sharing basis with demand processing. In either case, the problem is a simple one: can all the required operations be completed by the computer system within the schedules for their completion? For batch processing, the problem is represented on a composite schedule chart showing the operations required within a given interval, the estimated time required for each processing operation, and the time left for other processing as each higher-priority operation is added to the computer schedule. The estimates of time required for each operation will be refined during system design (if the study produces a decision to proceed) as the computer is chosen and the runs to be performed take shape. The initial scheduling analysis suggested here is comparable to job or production scheduling with existing or proposed facilities. It is most useful in determining whether a particular computer will satisfy the requirements to be imposed on it.

The scheduling problem for a demand processing system is only slightly more complex. Items handled by demand processing use a predictable amount of time each day, with a statistically predictable distribution through each day (and each week, if applicable). By allowing time for demand housekeeping (i.e., finding out what type of input item is presented for processing), a net remaining time and distribution is determined for intermixed batch processing. The schedule for this intermixed batch processing is then prepared as for a pure batch processing system.

Actually, the scheduling analysis for the demand portion of the system is much more critical. The computer system must be able to handle peak demand requirements, not just above-average demand loads. Accordingly, the study must determine accurately these peak demand load requirements (with a projection for anticipated growth in demand volume). If the resulting computer system is designed to accommodate all but the largest (and rarest) peak demand loads, it is likely to have adequate time available within each 24-hour period to handle most if not all batch processing that might be submitted to it. A scheduling analysis will clearly confirm or deny this likelihood, thus avoiding the possibility of later grief over inadequate capacity.

The documents to be analyzed during a feasibility study include the inputs to the area under study, the files and working papers used within that area, and the outputs from that area. All three categories will have counterparts in any computer system proposed to replace the current data processing system, although not all three categories will remain unchanged to the same degree in that system. Input documents usually change least, particularly if they originate outside the control of the company doing the processing. (But see the discussion in Chapter 3 under "Input Data Collection and Conversion.") With wider use of demand processing, input documents per se will be supplanted by input transmissions, held to input format requirements by the computer and its program.

Files and working papers are subject to the greatest change in a computer system because they are most likely to be absorbed within that system. Conversely, files and working papers are subject to the greatest discipline (i.e., rigorous definition as to content, format, extent, etc.) to meet the uncommon-sense requirements of a computer. These documents usually receive the most attention for possible consolidation, for as the number of different files is reduced, the feasibility of random access storage for files is increased, and the time required for file updating is usually reduced. In any case, the volume and variety of files needed for a computer system strongly affect its costs and efficiency, whether for batch or demand processing.

The analysis of output documents during the feasibility study is probably most crucial to its success; inputs and files establish constraints on the operation of a computer system; the needed outputs and their schedules determine the operations of the computer system. Distinctions should be drawn, however, among mandatory outputs (e.g., pay checks in a payroll application), optional or discretionary outputs (e.g, labor cost analyses by job), and occasional responses to queries. Mandatory outputs are just what their name implies, requirements of the application quite apart from the needs of management. The volume, extent, and frequency of production of these outputs represent additional constraints on a proposed computer system, like the constraints imposed by the inputs and files for the same application. Accordingly, mandatory output requirements need to be fully documented during the feasibility study. They are seldom changed much on conversion to a computer system, except for changes to a format for more efficient computer production, or a shorter schedule of production after closing off new inputs.

Occasional responses to queries are often overlooked during a feasibility study; yet they are most likely to be required in a computer system. As discussed earlier, the volume of responses to queries can be sharply reduced in a well-designed computer system by providing timely reports to management that forestall queries. Another reduction can be accomplished by absorbing into the computer system much of or all the process monitoring functions (e.g., expediting) that are performed outside the current processing system. Whether or not these reductions are accomplished eventually, the volume and variety of these queries and the work required to respond to them in the current system must be documented for a complete picture of that system. Without this information, the feasibility study risks inadequate pointers to improved system operation and to significant loads imposed on the current system.

The optional or discretionary outputs of a data processing system, its reporting system, offer room for the greatest improvements in conversion of the existing system. Computer speed can provide more current reports in shorter reporting periods. Computer decision making can eliminate some reports, or at least reduce their volume by excluding routine matters. New reports can be justified as useful and of little added cost by extracting pertinent management information from the input data needed to produce mandatory reports (e.g., labor cost analyses from the time cards submitted for payroll processing). With these and other opportunities for improvement, the feasibility study is well rewarded for concentration on the reporting system of current operations. Just as for the procedures used in current data processing, the study must document the current reporting system and evaluate its effectiveness. To do the latter, the study goes outside the processing system to the users of its reports. The study determines, at least roughly, the cost of each report, and then investigates its uses. If the report is similar to another one, users of the different reports are asked to evaluate for their needs the relative values of the two reports. If necessary, each user is asked about assuming the cost of production of the report he uses instead of using the other report or a compromise form. In addition, report users are approached for suggested improvements in current reports and to present ideas for more useful reports.

This survey of suggestions for reporting system improvements has much wider application for a feasibility study than is indicated by the foregoing discussion. A systems analyst brings to bear on the portion of the company selected for the study an unbiased, systems-oriented point of view. His fresh view is aided by his experience with comparable processing operations in other companies. However, the systems analyst cannot simply document these operations and thereby acquire the full breadth of knowledge about operations that exist within the company. He must be sensitive to niggling dissatisfactions with the way things are now done, as well as be alert to the wistfully described features that would be "nice" in a new system. His knowledge of computer capabilities allows him to separate the "nice" but expensive features (for management review) from the essential and the easily incorporated features of a new system. Using this approach, the study can uncover all desirable features for an optimum computer system while avoiding the expensive frills that could price the system beyond acceptance.

PROCEDURES FOR A FEASIBILITY STUDY

The procedures outlined here for a feasibility study are essentially an expansion of the preliminary survey discussed earlier in this chapter. While not inflexible, these procedures are the most effective for acquiring and codifying the information needed for the study. Three separate aspects of the study procedures are described: information flow analysis, reporting system analysis, and forms analysis. These aspects are obviously not separable in fact because they overlap each other. Rather, they are considered as three strands of a net, woven to collect all the needed information, overlapping to assure completeness of coverage.

An information flow analysis of a defined study area treats that area as a series of processing stations (or separate processing operations), accepting the division of functions that exists in the current system. The analysis follows the flow of information from its source, through each station, and to its ultimate destination outside the processing area, determining for each station the processing steps it performs and the facilities needed to perform them. This approach seems to de-emphasize the system approach. However, it is informed throughout by the analyst's systems-orientation, which pulls together the information he gathers into a system description. With this reservation understood, the information flow analysis procedures are given in interview form for a single station; they are equally useful in verifying the completeness of existing documentation. The questions to be answered for an information flow analysis include:

1. What input documents (or queries, or both) are received by this station? How many different kinds of input documents are received? (For example, for inventory control, item charge-outs, item receipts, advice of orders, changes to item descriptions; this aspect is also checked in forms analysis by collecting a complete set of forms and documents used in each operation.) Where do these different documents come from? How often and in what quantities are they received each time? What is the over-all volume of input documents received over

a week or a month, and how does this volume vary over that period?

2. What are the variations among the items of information on each kind of input document? Make up examples of all variations reported and confirm the completeness of the set. Get volume figures on each variation. (For example, for a mail-order input operation, the current catalogue and any previous catalogue from which orders will still be filled describe the variations of input items. Relative volume of orders from old catalogues is sufficient for a sales order processing analysis, whereas relative inventory activity is more important for an inventory control application.)

3. What processing is done with each kind of input document at this station? How long does each kind take to process? What personnel, files, equipment, or facilities are needed for each kind of processing?

(a) If information is taken from the document, how is this information used? What is done if some of the information is missing? How often is this necessary? How long does it take?

(b) If information is entered on the document, where does it come from? Calculations or files? (See below.) Administrative approval? How long does this take?

(c) If calculations are performed, what exactly are they? (Algebraic formulas are probably the clearest form of presentation; e.g., gross pay=hours × rate.) Are calculation tables or other aids used? If so, obtain copies of them and determine what went into their preparation. If calculating equipment is used, what are its costs and how fully is it being used? Are there features or drawbacks, or both, of the equipment that influence or determine the procedures of the station? Are any work sheets used in the calculations? (These work sheets, along with calculation tables and other aids, are also checked in forms analysis.)

(d) If files or other reference data are consulted for or affected by the processing at this station, what are they in detail? Are they on paper, on cards, in folders, or in someone's head? How is the appropriate file record located? How long does it take, on the average, to locate a record? Exactly what file information is used or affected by this operation? Who else uses this file? (This area is also investigated in detail in the forms analysis effort.)

(e) How vulnerable is this station's processing to errors in input or procedure? What is the relative volume of these errors or omissions? What control procedures are used to prevent or detect them? How are they corrected if found?

(f) Are there any company policies or external (e.g., legal, governmental, trade organization) requirements that govern the processing at this station? Are the procedures effective, or have they just developed from tradition? Are there any minor improvements or changes that might be suggested? Could a change in schedule of input deliveries or output requirements eliminate or minimize backlogs, offer more even use of the facilities and personnel at this step?

4. What are the outputs from this processing station? How many different kinds? How many of each kind over a normal processing period, and how does this volume vary over that period? Where do the outputs go? How many to each user and how often? (This output area is covered again by forms analysis and, in part, by the reporting system analysis.) What about responses to queries? How long does one take? How often are they needed?

As the systems analyst collects this information on each processing station, he applies it to the development of a system flow chart. This flow chart, annotated with volume, variation, and flow rate figures, shows the total information flow through the processing area under study. This flow chart also pinpoints bottlenecks in the current system, along with possible remedies for them. The analyst also develops more detailed flow charts (as needed) to depict calculations or other involved processing sequences, attaching to these detailed charts the annotated copies of all forms, records, tables, and aids that relate to the sequences they depict. (These annotated copies may come from the reporting system and forms analyses, or they may simply be duplicated here.) After he prepares his flow charts, he verifies their completeness and accuracy by mentally processing a document of each type through each step, with reference only to the procedures recorded on the flow charts and supporting papers. If he experiences uncertainties, he goes back to the questionable area for more information.

Concurrent with this information flow analysis, the systems analyst also examines the reporting system within the area under study. Initially, he may not distinguish between mandatory outputs and the optional or discretionary outputs that are truly reports to management. This initial lack of discrimination is unimportant, since the analysis corrects it. Further, the information gathered on mandatory outputs is needed for forms analysis, a process similar to reporting system analysis but with a broader scope and goal. During reporting system analysis, the following kinds of information are collected on each report or debatable output document:

1. What is the purpose of the report? Who or what group instituted it? How long ago? Why?
2. If the report is periodic, what period does it cover? What is the time lag between period closing and report delivery? If not periodic, what causes the report to be issued? How many such reports are issued per week, month, or year?
3. What organization or group prepares the report? What information sources are used? Does the preparer determine issuance of the report (e.g., summary of other reports)? What controls are used to assure completeness and accuracy of the report? How much does it cost to prepare the report (including materials, labor, equipment use, etc.)?
4. What is the report's distribution? How is each copy used? Is it retained in file, and if so, how long? Is each user satisfied with the report? If the report is not constrained by external requirements (e.g., government regulations, union contracts, trade organization agreements), what changes or shifts in reporting schedule would the user recommend? Can the user assess the report's value for him (i.e., accept budget responsibility for part of its cost of preparation)? If a similar report is also prepared, can the two (or more) be consolidated to the satisfaction of all users?

5. Does the report extract from its sources all information useful to management? Is the report concise enough to be useful (e.g., extraneous or trivial information left out)? Can supplementary information be provided easily? If the report is periodic, does it identify seasonal variations as such rather than as unexpected variations in company volume?

The results of this reporting system analysis are appended to the information flow analysis charts for review by management. Eventually, of course, the reporting system analysis will serve as the foundation for the design of an improved reporting system as part of the proposed computer system. Its function at this stage is to focus attention on this aspect of current operations.

The forms analysis aspect of the feasibility study is similar in many ways to the reporting system analysis. It goes beyond the reporting system analysis by covering every form, record, and working paper entered into, used within, or issued by the area under study. In a sense, therefore, the reporting system analysis is a subdivision of forms analysis. Forms analysis examines the "corpuscles" of information moving through the system considered in the information flow analysis: the items of information entering the system, circulating through it, being changed by it, or issued as outputs by it. The reporting system analysis concentrates on the discretionary outputs for management use, leaving the mandatory outputs for consideration by forms analysis. Of course this emphasis on system outputs, and on what is needed to produce them, is equally beneficial in forms analysis. With this approach, the necessary outputs and their sources are clearly identified for inclusion in the proposed computer system.

The initial step in forms analysis is simply the collection of a sample of every form, record, and working paper used in or submitted to the area under study (a step that can be performed as part of the preliminary study described earlier). The resulting collection often produces some surprises by its sheer quantity and by the number of duplications or overlaps. The collection's completeness must be verified, normally in the course of the information flow analysis. In addition, other information (much like that for the reporting system analysis) is needed for each form:

1. What is the purpose of the form? When was it instituted? By what group? Why?
2. What kind of form is it? Single or multipart? Handwritten or machine-prepared? Free or disciplined format? What is the cost of the unfilled-out form?
3. What information is entered on the form? What are the sizes and range of variation of each entry? (This query is complementary to the investigations during the information flow analysis. For computer system execution, this query requires answers as precise as the record layout diagram discussed in Chapter 3.)
4. What organization or group originates the form? What are the criteria for originating it? What sources of information are used in originating the form? How many of these forms are originated within a week, a month, or a year? What are the controls on its accuracy and completeness?
5. What is the form distribution (if there is more than one copy) or where does the form go from the originating group? Is some information added to the form? If so, by what group and from what sources?
6. What uses are made of the form by its recipients? What information is taken from the form by each user? For what purpose? Is the form retained in file? If so, how long? Why? Can this form be consolidated with other similar forms to simplify its origination or extension, or to extend its usefulness?

The information listed above is sufficient for forms used to transfer information from one group to another within the current operation. Other information is needed on forms that are part of a file for central reference, as given below:

1. How many forms or records are included in the file? Are all records in the file of the same format (and documented according to question 3 under forms analysis)? If not, what are the different formats?
2. What group is responsible for file maintenance and updating, or is more than one group active in changing this file? What

source documents are used in updating this file? Where do they originate? Is their accuracy under control? What is the schedule for updating the file? Is this often enough?

3. What groups use this file? What reports or forms are dependent on it? Is there a similar file that could be consolidated with this one? How would this affect the volume of the combined file? The procedures dependent on each file?

4. What is the over-all accuracy of the current file? Are the errors it contains damaging or costly (e.g., incorrect addresses in a mailing list, incurring return postage costs)?

5. What equipment, if any, is used to hold and employ the file? What is the cost of this equipment? What are the costs of labor and other facilities for file maintenance?

When the systems analyst has collected all the information indicated for forms analysis and for the files used in the area under study, he should have a complete picture of all operations conducted within that area. The picture includes the volume of data processed (together with short- and long-term variations in this volume), the schedule of current data processing, and the detailed costs of current data processing. This picture, already verified in detail by processing supervisors, also carries notes about possible improvements and simplifications for the area under study, together with questions for management review of objectives and the means to achieve them within that area. The analyst will also have in mind (if not on paper) at this stage the main features of a computer system to handle most of this processing. The correct word is "most" and not "all" for two reasons. Some data processing will fall outside the computer system (e.g., input editing), preceding submission of the data for computer processing. Other data, notably exceptional items of low volume and high complexity of processing, will be left aside for later decision on their inclusion in the computer system; during system design, these exceptional items may prove to be complexes of unexceptional elements.

The analyst cannot (and should not) finalize his ideas for a proposed computer system until he has reviewed with management: (1) his questions on objectives and means; (2) the range of normal, as opposed to exceptional, items for handling within the computer system; (3) the mandatory computer features for the system, in contrast to features that may or may not be justifiable; and (4) a projection on volume growth within the area under consideration over the useful life of the proposed computer system, along with some estimate of the surplus (for this application) computer capacity needed to accommodate other applications. Therefore, the final stage of the feasibility study involves management review of current system documentation, redefinition of objectives in the area under study, and general guidance for the analyst in his development of a proposed computer system.

MANAGEMENT REVIEW

Management review of the systems analyst's work applies management experience in directing the area and in using its output to the task of redefining its goals. Almost incidentally, the review allows management to assess the analyst's penetration into the area under study, his absorption of the vocabulary it employs, and of the unique requirements it must satisfy. A thorough study will penetrate the processing area to a depth of detail that exceeds management knowledge of the area, a fact that should not confuse management evaluation of the analyst's work. As part of this assessment, management should expect to see a system flow chart, detailed flow charts, procedural descriptions, schedule requirements, and document descriptions. If for no other reason, management must examine this documentation to confirm the inclusion of all requirements and constraints on the area under study.

The review by management is most fruitful in considering explicit policy restrictions and implicit or traditional restrictions on current processing. Often, these restrictions no longer reflect management policies; in fact, the "policies" reflected in current processing may come as a surprise. Their confirmation, or denial and modification, by management must be conveyed precisely to the analyst for incorporation into the proposed computer system. The review must also establish that external requirements (e.g., those imposed by government) are satisfied. In addition, management can complete the purging of inconsistencies and duplications that the analyst could not resolve at a lower level.

During management review, the objectives of the area under study are subject to redefinition within the limit of computer capabilities. In addition, the means to achieve these goals are evaluated. The systems analyst supports both efforts. He offers explanations of computer capabilities as necessary for redefinition of objectives. He supplies relative cost figures of computer system features for evaluation of the means for achievement of these objectives. His cost figures need not be firm, nor need management decisions on these features be final. Rather, management can compare the advantages of a particular feature (a nonmandatory one) with its cost to decide whether it should be included or reserved for later decision. The feasibility study merely starts the process of developing a computer system without fixing its configuration. The study establishes the essential requirements to be met by a computer system, thereby allowing a rough determination of its cost. With this information, management can decide intelligently whether to invest in further development efforts without being committed irrevocably to the use of a computer.

The end product of this management review is a confirmed description of system objectives and of the requirements to be met by the system. This description includes detailed information about. the volume of data to be processed (including projected growth) and the required processing schedule. At this point, management lacks only cost figures for a proposed computer system so as to make its decision to proceed with system design or to reject it. Yet, at this stage, management has an adequate and accurate basis for obtaining these figures, as well as having more accurate figures on current processing costs. As a bonus, management has complete documentation of the procedures used within the study area, pointers to savings and improvements in that area, and the benefits of the re-evaluation of the area and its objectives. The first phase of the application of computer "logic" to the area under study has been completed.

6

THE USES OF A
FEASIBILITY STUDY

The pattern for a feasibility study laid out in the preceding chapter leaves unanswered the question that triggers the study; i.e., to computerize or not to computerize. The study develops all the information needed to pose that question accurately, along with the background to evaluate the answers it evokes, but omits the essential ingredient for a management decision on the question—the cost of a proposed computer system. This ingredient can be supplied by the systems analyst, in view of his support of the management review at the end of the study, although he may not be the best source for this information.

The systems analyst probably has more information than is necessary or desirable for an unbiased determination of proposed computer system costs. He knows the cost of current operations, and having a vested interest in the adoption of a computer system (whether he is a company employee or is from an outside service), may be tempted to pare his estimate for a more favorable comparison with current costs. On the other hand, the analyst may not have enough information to come up with the best estimate of computer system costs. He may not have a wide enough knowledge of different computers or of the available part-time computer facilities to select the optimum supplier for this system; if so, his estimate of computer system costs will be higher than it should be. In either case, "outsider" estimates and suggestions are of considerable value at this stage.

The problem then arises as to the selection of "outsiders" who will furnish cost estimates and suggestions for a proposed computer system. First, management should select the most promising approaches to computer system implementation, based on advice from the systems analyst. Then, all accessible suppliers for those approaches should be solicited. The various approaches to implementation of a computer system include the following (in order of decreasing capacity):

1. A complete on-premises computer system, using demand processing, batch processing, or a mix of both
2. An equivalent system with most elements (and their problems) off-premises at a computer center, using the computer on a time-shared basis, which makes it seem like exclusive service
3. A reduced system that may retain data collection and conversion on-premises (but may not), with time rental of an off-premises computer for only batch processing
4. A composite system that uses business equipment for basic processing operations, developing by-product computer-readable data for off-premises computer preparation of reports, etc.

At least two of these approaches should be investigated in some detail, preferably with the aid of competitive suppliers for each approach being considered. In fact, management may find it worthwhile to solicit responses for all four approaches (as well as for any others that may seem useful for the area under study). If any question exists as to whether or not to solicit a proposal, decide in favor of doing so.

Having made its selections, management solicits preliminary proposals from suppliers by making available all feasibility study results except current operation costs and personnel loading. These results include the proposed system procedures (revised from current procedures to eliminate duplication and effect consolidations approved during management review), supported by full descriptions of forms, records, and files, by detailed breakdowns of data volume by item type, and by required processing schedules.

Above all, the solicitation describes the objectives approved for the proposed system, the agreed-on mandatory features, and the optional features for separate consideration.

With this documentation prepared, it is presented to the selected sources as the basis for preliminary proposals. If an on-premises computer system is being considered, several computer manufacturers are invited to propose the system. If the system may use off-premises computer facilities, the computer centers within easy access are asked for proposals. If a composite system is under consideration, several business machine manufacturers should be approached for proposals; the data they supply will serve as source material for proposals by computer centers for the coordinate functions they are to perform.

It is important to remember that these proposals can be only preliminary because they lack the detailed base provided by system design. However, these preliminary proposals bring to light ideas and approaches that might otherwise be overlooked. Of more immediate importance, these proposals offer unbiased (albeit possibly too optimistic) cost figures on a proposed computer system, supplying the missing ingredient for a management decision on the basic question. On a longer range basis, the solicitation weeds out those potential suppliers who do not respond to it, narrowing the field to those willing to assist in further investigation.

A preliminary proposal should include a clear description of the equipment or services offered to meet the requirements stated in the solicitation, complete cost information for each element suggested, the portion of the over-all computer system implemented, and the schedule of processing that can be maintained. Different sources will offer this information in different ways in their proposals. It is essential that they provide all this information if their proposal is to receive a valid appraisal. For example, the proposal from a computer manufacturer should specify all the equipment he recommends, all the optional or special features (which cost extra), and the cost figures for each item. To make this information meaningful, the proposal should also spell out how much of the computer system is supplied by these recommendations; i.e., what operations shown on the system flow chart are handled by the recommended equipment and what operations are not. In addition, the proposal should include a tentative processing schedule to demonstrate that the recommended equipment will satisfy schedule requirements and to show the unused capacity for other applications.

A preliminary proposal from a computer center may differ considerably from both computer manufacturers' proposals and the proposals from other computer centers. A computer center proposal may cover only the data processing operations needed for the computer system, either with or without data conversion. At the other extreme, the proposal may also include in the same package a part of system design, programming, and the conversion of company files for computer processing. Here again the proposal cannot be evaluated unless its elements are spelled out and priced separately. More important, it is only the processing costs (and data conversion costs, if the computer center is to perform that function) that have any bearing on the feasibility question; the other cost elements on which a computer center might propose are not pertinent until computer processing is deemed feasible for the application under study. (These other cost elements are considered in succeeding sections of this book.)

A preliminary proposal from a business equipment manufacturer should be like that from a computer manufacturer except for its restricted scope. (The solicitation of business equipment manufacturers must make clear that this restricted scope is acceptable.) A proposal from this source should specify the number of units of each type (as well as their price) needed to handle the volume of data indicated in the solicitation, their effective (as opposed to maximum) processing speed for the application described, and the form of computer-readable data that they produce. Proposals from business equipment manufacturers usually require secondary solicitations of computer centers for the costs of processing not performed by the business equipment. Since all solicitations are intended to unearth ideas as well as cost estimates, these secondary solicitations should provide a complete picture of over-all computer system requirements without, however, giving clues as to current or proposed system costs. For example, a secondary solicitation can provide all the information supplied in a primary solicitation, indicating only the portion of the over-all system to be implemented by business machines, not their number. In addition, the secondary solicitation should describe the form of data produced by the business machines and the volume and schedule of production; the schedule requirements for computer center production of reports should be unchanged from the primary solicitation.

After proposals have been received from all possible sources, they must be evaluated against the stipulations of the solicitation, as well as for usefulness in the light of the requirements indicated above. Since these are informal proposals rather than sealed bids, additional information or clarification of a proposal should be requested if it seems promising but is incomplete or unclear. In addition, if any proposed implementation depends on equipment or services from other suppliers (e.g., data communications via common carrier such as Bell System or Western Union), these suppliers should be solicited for their suggestions and cost figures pertaining to their contribution to the over-all system. The systems analyst is an obvious candidate for performance of this evaluation and follow-through.

Eventually, all the suggestions and cost figures from "outsiders" will be gathered, still without completing the final ingredient for a management decision—the estimated cost of a computer system. Instead, there will be partial cost figures covering a variety of approaches, each approach offering certain advantages and certain drawbacks or limitations. At this point, the systems analyst should have developed some rating of the various approaches, whether formal or not; he should be able to select the "de luxe" and "economy" approaches from each type of source (computer manufacturer, computer center, or business equipment manufacturer). For each selection, the analyst arrives at a complete operating cost figure by adding to the costs included in the proposal those costs of unchanged current operations and estimates of other costs (e.g., labor for operation of the computer or business machines). When the analyst presents these complete operating cost estimates, he supplies management with the final ingredient for its decision.

The decision required of management is not that of selecting one approach from among the alternatives presented by the systems analyst. Rather, management must decide whether to investigate further the potentials of computer (or business equipment) data processing, basing this decision almost entirely on cost comparisons. If the costs of current processing within the area under study are bracketed by the cost figures for the "de luxe" and "economy" approaches of a particular type, the decision is clearly to proceed with further investigation. True, the over-all costs of a new system are raised by the conversion expenses (no matter how long the period over which they are written off); yet this bracketing strongly indicates that the new system can be profitable. However, when the operating cost figures for a possible new system equal or exceed current operating costs, other considerations must enter into the decision.

A proposed new system that offers unused capacity to accommodate other applications at little or no additional cost can justify further investigation even if the "economy" version of ths new system costs more to run than do current operations. The question is: How much more? If the proposed new system includes an on-premises computer, its unused capacity is likely to be rather large, a factor reflected in the rating by the systems analyst. (A computer's *utilization factor*, the ratio of time used to time available, is a measure of efficiency, not feasibility.) Accordingly, further investigation for an on-premises computer system may be justified, if enough other applications await conversion to computer processing, when its estimated operating costs exceed current processing costs by more than 50 per cent. In many successful computer installations, current expenses for the first application were only 60 per cent of projected computer system costs.

The other sources of computer system capabilities (computer centers and business equipment in composite systems) offer little or no unused capacity for additional applications, since their operating costs tend to rise in direct proportion to the volume of data they handle. As a result, an application too small to justify an on-premises computer narrows the ground for justification of another source. However, if there is no single application that justifies an on-premises computer, the combination of applications with appreciable volume in the company may do so. Accordingly, a single application being considered for computer center processing can be carried beyond the feasibility study stage, even with unfavorable cost estimates, as a test and educational case; better still, the feasibility study can be extended to include other applications. In either case, most computer centers are quite willing to provide "on-the-job" training and direct experience in using a computer data processing system. This extension capability to justify an on-premises computer may be offset by the advantages of leaving computer problems to the computer experts at the center.

A composite system, using business equipment for basic data processing, offers no real potential for extension to other applications at little or no additional cost. Therefore, the composite system must show advantages either in savings on current processing or in better reporting for management, to justify a management decision to proceed with the investigation. One application that justified conversion to a composite system had as current expenses some $7,000 per month for a punched-card or tabulator processing system, including labor. Projected costs for the composite system included $230 per month for on-premises bookkeeping machines with perforated tape output (again including labor), plus some $560 per month for off-premises computer services in preparing detailed reports that were returned two days after the closing of a monthly reporting period, in contrast to the reports on a six-month period delivered two months after closing by the existing system. Obviously, this application could fully justify conversion on both counts.

As a final note, management must realize what further investigation, beyond the feasibility study, can yield. If the feasibility study represents the first phase of applying computer "logic" to current operations, system design is the second and most intensive phase of this application. The system design effort is devoted to the mating of improved data processing with the facilities that allow that improvement. As such, the system design effort will provide a processing system of greater value to management but not lower cost. On the contrary, system design is most likely to develop a more expensive processing system than those proposed in response to the results of the feasibility study. System design yields multifold returns from these additions to the operating expenses for the new system, if only from improvements in management control of company operations within the application area. Accordingly, if management can see any prospect of profitable use of computer capabilities (based on the feasibility study and its uses as outlined in this chapter), the additional investment in a system design effort is justified; i.e., the basic decision should be to proceed.

PART III

SYSTEM DESIGN

A feasibility study usually provides the impetus for development of a computer system, but stops far short of its design if only for reasons of economy. The study documents what and how much is now being done and why it is done. System design goes on to determine what should be done and how best to do it. System design begins by applying computer "logic" to the study area to develop a new system plan that fulfills all current area requirements and goals, including the redefined ones. After this plan is approved by management, it is particularized to match those features of the computer systems or other facilities being considered for its implementation. Specifically, this phase of system design establishes the scope of the implementation scheme for the new system plan, determining at the same time how much is to be left for manual processing. This modified new system plan (or plans) supports the choice of approach, if not yet made, and of the specific facilities or services to implement it. After this choice is made, system design refines its plan to reap any special advantages offered by the selected implementation.

This description of the system design effort separates it from the facility selection task (and the two are treated in separate chapters), but the two efforts are actually complementary. The new system plan will anticipate computer or other improved processing without commitment to a single approach, unless one was chosen as a result of the feasibility study. As the facilities offered by alternative approaches or sources, or both, are measured against plan requirements, the plan itself becomes more precise, focusing on the capabilities of those sources still in contention. These parallel efforts continue until the final plan is evolved as an exact match with the selected facilities, exploiting the strengths and compensating for any weaknesses.

A suggestion often made when a company first considers computer processing is that conversion be done in two steps, first to a punched-card or other business equipment system, and then from there to a computer system. This two-step approach assumes that the first conversion is both easier and cheaper than direct conversion to a computer system and that this first step simplifies the second one. Unfortunately, neither assumption is necessarily true. Any conversion step disrupts normal operations and imposes first-time costs. Why assume two such burdens when one, which is likely to be less costly than the sum of the two, is sufficient? Further, as discussed in Chapter 6, a punched-card or business equipment system is least capable of expansion for additional applications. Consequently, this approach should be chosen on its own merits, not because other approaches are infeasible. If an application potentially justifies a computer system, but a "foot-wetting" approach is desired, it may be better to use a computer center for processing of the application, provided the advantages and drawbacks of its services are understood.

The equipment manufacturers and computer centers being considered for implementation of the new system plan offer assistance that varies in value as the system design effort proceeds. Their preliminary proposals submitted after the feasibility study will normally indicate the support they offer and its cost, if any, as well as ideas or suggestions for the new system plan. Apart from these ideas and suggestions, this support is of little value during the initial phase of system design. As the field of choice narrows, this support becomes more valuable in mating the system design to the capabilities offered for its implementation. After a sole supplier is chosen, extensive use should be made of his support because it is then vital. The degree of support offered by each supplier is an important factor in the selection process.

When the system design effort is completed and the implementing facility is selected, management will have complete plans and cost figures for the new processing system. Much remains to be done in converting to the new system, yet these conversion steps and their costs should be well defined in the system design. Thus, the completion of system design is a natural breakpoint for management review and decision to continue or terminate the conversion process. Management participation is essential to the system design effort, both to provide the decisions contributing to it and to avoid being overwhelmed at its conclusion. However, the review at this breakpoint is particularly important, since later changes to system design will be more costly and will involve modifications of structures (e.g., programs, procedures) rather than of the blueprints from which they are built.

7

THE PATTERN OF SYSTEM DESIGN

Like the feasibility study, a system design effort varies to match the company and application being considered, but it, too, displays a general pattern beneath these differences. This pattern brings to bear on the study area the full impact of the *system* approach, considering the whole while designing its parts. System design starts with the development of a functional plan for a new system that satisfies the goals and requirements established by the feasibility study while ignoring current organization and procedures within the study area. This functional plan for a new, integrated system cuts across current organizational lines, pulling together the elements that are now fragmented or decentralized. If management has not yet selected the most promising approach to computer utilization, this functional plan will assist in making that selection by determining more exactly the requirements for an optimum system and its implementation. If the approach has already been selected, the functional plan is made more specific, to reflect the special capabilities and limitations (if any) of that approach and thereby assist in the choice of the sole supplier.

Finally, upon selection of the supplier and the facility (or service by a computer center) to be used in implementing the system, system design particularizes its plan to accommodate both the advantages and disadvantages of the selection. The end result of this process is a total system design for the application being considered, within the reasonable limits imposed by costs and the arbitrary limits imposed by the selected equipment or service.

The bulk of this chapter treats the system design effort in more detail so that management may appreciate the process. The chapter begins with a description of the ground rules for a system design effort.

GROUND RULES FOR SYSTEM DESIGN

As will be seen, system design procedures are less readily defined than are those for a feasibility study, reflecting perhaps the creative aspect of system design. Similarly, the ground rules are less defined than those for a feasibility study, but they are similar. The scope of the system design effort is normally the same as that for the preceding feasibility study, requiring no further consideration. Only a naturally related application that is not currently performed or performed so little that it does not justify study can be added to the system design scope without a prior feasibility study. Even then, the added application must be scrutinized closely to avoid the introduction of a host of exceptional processing operations.

The schedule for system design depends strongly on the results of the feasibility study. If the study has led to selection of one approach for the new system, the initial phase can proceed directly to particularization of its system plan to match that approach. If not, the initial phase must be scheduled to allow for approach selection. In either case, the schedule should allow enough time for a useful effort while precluding unnecessary activities. Although not typical, one company allocated three calendar years for its feasibility study and system design effort before selecting a computer system that was to replace its first computer system; in retrospect, the company feels that its caution was well rewarded.

The most crucial ground rule for a system design effort, as for a feasibility study, concerns its reporting and participation level within the company. Application of the *system* approach to processing within the study area will pose questions that can be resolved only by top management. The changes proposed to meet the goals set at that level may be so different from current operations as to require confirmation at that level. Of equal importance, the total investment needed to carry through the results of the system design effort will demand a final decision by top management. Management is well advised to participate in the process that leads up to this decision point if it is not to be buried in a mass of detail at that point. Management need not get bogged down in the day-to-day efforts of the systems analyst, but should review his results periodically, if only to catch unacceptable features before they become irremovable. Since a major objective of system design is the creation of a management tool (which also performs mandatory processing), management participation seems well justified.

INITIAL SYSTEM DESIGN

The initial phase of system design is sometimes called the *solution concept* phase, in conformity with the problem definition aspect of the feasibility study. This phase starts from the documentation of inputs, required outputs, and redefined management goals of the study area, but ignores current organization and processing procedures in designing a new system to satisfy its requirements. This initial phase may precede selection of the computer utilization approach. The solution concept is independent of its implementation, but contributes to the selection of the implementing approach. On the other hand, a choice made prior to development of the initial system design allows an earlier transition to the detailed phases.

A systems analyst begins initial system design by considering the new system as a *black box;* i.e., something with unknown contents which, in accordance with its over-all goals, produces the required outputs when the specified inputs are supplied. This black box is divided up, in turn, into several smaller black boxes by analyzing the system and identifying a set of isolable functions or subsystems that together satisfy all system requirements. The analysis may further subdivide some of or all these functional elements into sub-elements for separate consideration. Whatever the depth, this analysis reveals the functions essential to the system and the interactions among them. Like the outline of a speech, this analysis may never be formally documented, yet it underlies the whole system design effort. This analysis (often an informal product of the feasibility study) from the top down of the area under study exposes its inherent "logical" structure. The system design effort then develops an efficient and economical realization of this "logical" structure.

The solution concept "outline" that results from analysis must be filled in before it can be realized. Surprisingly, perhaps, the design effort can best start from the required outputs and reports, working backward from there to the specified inputs. This backward approach is most conducive to development of a management information system that is integral with the basic data processing system. With this goal in mind, and guided by his outline of the new system "logical" structure, the analyst builds on paper a new system plan that combines the best features of the current system with other features made possible by improved processing facilities. He includes only those current procedures that are efficient, redesigning or eliminating others which detract from system effectiveness. The procedures are selected or designed in anticipation of computer processing, but are left in generalized form to allow other implementations. The analyst also determines file requirements and information flow paths for the new system. As he develops these flow paths, the analyst investigates the information for its pertinence to improved management control. When appropriate, he proposes new or better reports for management, adding inputs to the system for these reports if they seem justified.

Management participation is essential throughout this most creative portion of system design. The analyst tries to consolidate separate operations, standardize different operations, and eliminate unnecessary or duplicated operations in the current system as he transposes its elements into his new system plan. At the same time, the analyst recommends new operations for improved management support by the new system. Fundamentally, the new system must duplicate the mandatory results of the current system, but need not duplicate the system itself. The analyst may try to eliminate essential operations of the current system because he fails to recognize their necessity, a failure that is prevented by management participation in the design effort. At the other extreme, the analyst may include unjustifiable features or refinements in the new system if he is not closely supervised by management throughout this phase of system design.

For both extremes, the documentation of the current system by the feasibility study affords an excellent cross-check of the analyst's plans. When he wishes to consolidate, standardize, or eliminate a current procedure, he should identify it to management and compare it with his proposed replacement for management approval before the change is made final. (The stock answer of "it simplifies computer processing" can be parried by demanding a clear explanation of the resulting simplification.) Similarly, when the analyst recommends an additional procedure, input, or report, he should indicate both the value and the costs of his proposed addition. Particularly for additional procedures, the analyst should identify the inputs and files already in the current system to support them, as well as the added inputs and files they require.

Many changes that the analyst recommends are intended to make the new system conform more closely to the application's "logical" structure; these changes will generally be simplifications of current processing. Other changes arise from redefined company goals for the application area, either developed during the feasibility study or recognized during management participation in system design; these changes should be identified as such when the analyst presents them for management review. Still other recommended changes, while related to redefined goals, may stem more directly from the implicit goal of improved management reporting. These changes will show up principally in the system output area, but may thread back through the entire system plan. One example of a change that takes the latter form is *classification coding;* i.e., item or account code numbers that indicate the outputs affected by the transaction as well as identifying the transaction source. This type of *significance coding* (meaningful identification codes as opposed to arbitrary codes), which is essential for multiple-category demand processing, permits improved reporting in a batch processing system by simplifying the sorting of input items for any desired report. The advantages of this change become clearer when the new system is examined first in terms of its output reports and then traced back to its input specifications, stressing the mandatory outputs and management reports.

Another example of a change to improve reporting for management supports the idea of *management by exception* (discussed in

Chapter 4). This idea is realized by establishing criteria to distinguish between expected and unusual entries or processing results. With these criteria and the procedures to apply them built into the new system plan, detailed reports to management will not present the expected results, although their effects will be reflected in the report summary of results. Instead, the detailed reports will show only the exceptional results, those which demand management attention. The report user is thereby spared the task of leafing through a "five-foot shelf" report to extract the five pages (or, even worse, the five lines) of important information it contains.

These criteria can also be applied to trigger "flag" reports of exceptional entries or results for immediate management attention. These "flag" reports can be produced without delay by a demand processing system, but the situation is a bit different in batch processing. An exceptional entry can trigger a "flag" report from a batch processing system without delay; an exceptional result must await processing before it is produced and can trigger a report. This limitation is not too serious because entries are processed as far as possible when first submitted to a batch processing system.

The reporting system in the new system plan should provide faster reporting of shorter periods if the shorter periods match normal business cycles and the reports serve definite needs. For a manufacturing company with a six-week production cycle, the reporting system should produce a six-week summary report on each cycle in addition to weekly (or pay period) trend indication reports, monthly summaries for accounting functions on that cycle (e.g., accounts payable), and the usual quarterly and annual reports. Each report should be designed for use, not to show how much information it can contain. Exception reporting, just described, does much to reduce the bulk and increase the usefulness of a report.

Another, less far reaching technique is to provide only summary results in a report unless more complete information is requested. Still another technique supplements current results with comparison information (e.g., last year's sales figures or the projections for this year over the same reporting period, together with the percentage deviation of the actual from the expected result). This comparison information at least distinguishes a normal seasonal slump from a disastrous change in the business picture. Better still, it is adaptable to exception reporting by suppressing results that differ insignificantly from expectation, leaving in the report only those results whose deviations need management attention.

When historical data or even experience with an application is unavailable as a basis for projection, comparison information can be produced by projection methods such as PERT (Program Evaluation and Review Technique, developed by the U.S. Navy for its Polaris program). It should be apparent from the preceding discussion that management must assist in designing the reporting system if it is to get a useful tool rather than a blizzard of what becomes scrap paper as soon as it is produced.

Management must also contribute to this creative phase of system design by suggesting its own ideas for better managerial control of the application. The system developed on paper during this phase is more tolerant of changes than its later versions will be. It is better to delve into odd corners now, before the new system takes firm shape, than it is to risk the wastage that these questions may cause later on. For example, the features left as optional by the feasibility study deserve re-examination in the context of the new system plan. As always, the value of an improvement must be weighed against its costs before a decision is made. However, since the analyst is estimating both values and costs at this stage, a marginal decision (i.e., on a feature that is almost but not quite justified) can be delayed for later consideration when more exact estimates are available.

At the conclusion of the solution concept phase, management and the analyst will have agreed on a new system plan for the application under study and on its major (but not all) features. If no approach to computer utilization has yet been selected, the new system plan is left general enough to allow its implementation by any of the approaches being considered. Otherwise, the plan includes only those features offered by the selected approach, thereby overlapping the next phase of system design. Whether it does or does not remain general, the new system plan is "computerized" in its reorganization and centralization of currently separate operations, the result of applying computer "logic" to the processing area. All succeeding system design activities to realize the benefits of that "logic" are based firmly on this new system plan.

APPROACH SELECTION

Approach selection is a natural continuation of initial system design, in the sense that it makes the new system plan more explicit. The new system plan establishes what is to be done to process the application under study. This continuation determines how much of the processing is to be done by the new approach and, if necessary, selects the approach from among those still under consideration. The extent of implementation of the new system plan by an approach (e.g., how much of the system is handled by the computer?) determines its cost-to-advantage ratio, which in turn contributes to the choice between alternative approaches. Accordingly, both aspects of selection are discussed here even though only the first may be necessary if the approach has already been selected.

The approaches to be considered here differ somewhat from those discussed in Chapter 6. For example, no distinction need be made initially between on-premises and off-premises computer facilities. Instead, batch processing and demand (or mixed demand and batch) processing should be investigated as alternative approaches, leaving the choice of computer location for later decision. The selected approach may preclude the use of off-premises facilities, automatically answering the secondary question. Similarly, an approach using business equipment need not be subdivided into one that uses outside computer processing and another that does not, since the investigation into extent of implementation will consider this problem.

To determine how much of the new system plan can be handled economically by a particular approach, the systems analyst must particularize the plan to match the features of that approach. He then performs a series of *trade-off studies*, balancing the advantages of one realization of a system black box (isolable function) against its effects on the rest of the system. In these studies, he considers both the interactions among the system functions and their relative importance to the over-all system. For example, the analyst must choose between centralized and decentralized data conversion for a computer system, but he cannot base his choice solely on the merits of these alternatives. The better choice, when considered alone, may have so adverse an effect on a more important system function as to be the poorer choice for this application. To illustrate this fact, realize that centralized data conversion can cripple a demand processing system by effectively batching those transactions which should be entered as soon as they arrive for processing.

Management will be involved in many of the decisions needed in these trade-off studies. Specifically, management is asked to compare intangible benefits such as improved reporting, faster processing, or better customer service against the cost of realizing them. These evaluations are crucial in determining the extent of implementation of the new system plan by the approach under consideration. As an example of these needed evaluations by management, consider the extension of a batch processing system through decentralized data conversion and collection. Can the costs of this extension be justified by the value of earlier data capture and the reduction in transcription errors, or should current data collection channels be retained to feed into the computer system through a centralized conversion function? The analyst will present other factors which bear on this decision, but it is ultimately a management decision.

The end product of these trade-off studies is an optimum system design for the approach being studied. This design is more specific than the new system plan, yet is still broad enough to accommodate most suppliers for that approach. The optimum system design identifies the portion of the over-all system to be handled by the approach in question, along with the processing volumes and schedules to be met as well as input, file, and report requirements, if not specific layouts. The procedures to be executed by this portion of the system may not be defined exactly if different suppliers offer different features, but the processing requirements are established quite clearly. To assist in comparative evaluation of the design, it should be accompanied by an estimate of over-all system operating costs (excluding first-time costs and cost write-offs) together with a description of the advantages it has over other approaches or the current system, or over both.

When more than one approach is in contention during this phase, an optimum system design is developed for each. This development process often rules out an approach before the design is completed, by demonstrating that the costs outweigh the advantages. If not, the surviving designs are compared along with their costs and advantages for a management selection of the best justifiable design. This step completes the approach selection phase except possibly for a choice between on- and off-premises computer facilities. This choice may not be forced by the optimum system design, leaving computer manufacturers and computer centers on a par as possible suppliers for the new system, an unlikely circumstance. The choice of computer location carries with it the choice between an off-premises service and an on-premises facility with its attendant personnel and space requirements. To facilitate this management choice, a discussion of these alternative sources is given here.

ON-PREMISES VERSUS OFF-PREMISES FACILITIES

Several factors that affect the choice between on- and off-premises computer facilities have already been discussed, albeit rather briefly. Still to be described are the facilities and services offered by a computer center. If the center is fully staffed and equipped, it can offer services ranging from systems analysis through programming and on into data conversion and computer processing. Most computer centers emphasize one or another portion of this range. Some of them specialize in programming, supplementing (or substituting for) the programming staffs of computer users. Others concentrate on rental of their computer facilities and offer those services (e.g., programming, data conversion) that contribute to this goal. A computer rental center can process the by-product data from a business equipment system or handle the overloads from an on-premises computer. It can also be used in place of an on-premises computer system, but certain precautions must be observed to use the computer center properly.

Use of a computer for an application involves four cost elements, whether the computer is on or off premises:

1. Programming
2. File conversion (for an application to be run more than once)
3. Input data conversion (e.g., key punching)
4. Processing or machine-time costs

File conversion and continuing data conversion costs are about the same, whether performed on premises or by a computer center. Input data conversion is often kept on premises, even when processing is performed at a computer center, to get validity checks on the data. On-premises personnel handle the same type of record constantly and can catch absurdities that might pass unnoticed at the center. Data conversion as a by-product of business machine processing or of data communications is an excellent way of achieving this goal.

A computer center may well offer lower processing costs than can be attained in on-premises processing, particularly for the first application on a new system. The center runs its machines close to 24 hours a day, seven days a week, to realize a low cost-per-hour figure for computer time. However, the total processing cost rises with volume for a computer center user, whereas the cost of an application on an on-premises system decreases as other applications are put on the computer. This is, of course, another way of stating the growth potential of an on-premises computer system. If the computer is justified for one application, additional applications can be processed "without cost," or they can assume part of the cost from the original application.

A computer center can quote a significantly lower first-time programming cost for an application it is to process regularly. Unless the user specifies otherwise, the center retains ownership of the programs it writes for its clients. If the center owns a program for a similar application, its low price stems from modification of that program for the new application. Both clients are protected because the center treats both the original and the modified program as proprietary items. With no similar program in its files, the new program still borrows heavily from other programs, to hold down costs. In either case, the program is usually written in machine language to conserve processing time. This saved time represents money to the center, particularly if a fixed fee or a rate-per-input item is quoted for processing. Machine-language programming ties the program to the computer at the center, just as the center's ownership of the program ties in the application. The user is responsible for the costs of any changes he may request, but the center is responsible for reprogramming if it switches to a new computer.

A computer center user preserves greater freedom of action, at the expense of higher programming costs, by requiring ownership of the program and master files for his application prior to his entering into agreement with the center. When he does this, the user splits the center's function into two tasks, one using the center's programming services and the other independently using its processing facilities. To get full value from program ownership, the user must obtain adequate program documentation and operation (run) manuals. He may also specify that the program be written in a machine-independent language (e.g., COBOL), thus avoiding commitment to the computer at that center. This choice can reduce programming time and documentation costs, but may increase processing costs. When the user owns his program, he assumes responsibility for reprogramming costs if the center changes to a new computer. These costs are small if his program is written in a machine-independent language. More important, he is free to shift the application to another center or to his own computer. Finally, program ownership allows treatment of its cost as a capital investment rather than a straight expense.

The separation of programming from processing services is imperative if the computer center is being used on an interim basis because otherwise, the programming cost is not recoverable when the user shifts to his own computer. Programming support by the supplier of an on-premises computer is enhanced by the existence of a satisfactorily programmed application. The existing program establishes standards to which the programming support effort can conform, thus simplifying or eliminating the task of standards development. The existing program also augments the programs developed with the manufacturer's support for starting the computer system at a higher utilization factor (ratio of time used to time available on the computer). Conversely, if a user places a short-term application with a computer center, the separate task approach is unjustified because of the higher programming costs it entails.

The major drawback in the use of computer rental centers for batch processing stems from the scheduling restrictions imposed on the user. (Time-shared access to a computer center avoids the scheduling restriction, but may substitute a restriction on processing volume.) Low-volume users of computer rental centers often complain (justly or not) that their applications are shunted aside in favor of larger clients, making fulfillment of their schedule requirements marginal at best. Along this line, penalties for nonfulfillment are difficult to apply even if the computer center agrees to their inclusion in a contract for service. It is true that use of a computer center relieves the user of staffing and administering an on-premises system. However, retention of data conversion as an on-premises function implies administration. Conversely, availability of programming services reduces the staffing requirements for an on-premises system (although some on-premises programming capabilities make an on-premises system more responsive to user needs).

To summarize, a computer rental center must be used, if processing volume does not justify an on-premises computer, to obtain the benefits of faster processing. When processing volume is almost large enough to justify an on-premises computer, a computer rental center may be used to gain experience with computer processing. In both cases, the user is advised to guard against the possible pitfalls of this approach, namely, being locked into the computer center, being ignored in favor of larger clients, or simply being misserviced. When an on-premises computer can definitely be justified, management must choose between the flexibility of an on-premises system plus its requisite supporting staff (with or without a full programming staff) and the economies with restrictions offered by a computer rental center.

SHARING, TIME BROKERS, AND OTHER OFF-PREMISES FACILITIES

Computer rental centers are not the only sources for off-premises computer facilities. A computer user with idle time on his machine may offer that time at or below his cost, to reduce the expenses of his own operations. Enough surplus time of this kind is available in larger cities to support the activities of *time brokers*, companies that buy surplus time at wholesale to resell it in smaller parcels at retail rates. Some computer rental centers engage in time brokering to supplement their own machine capacity. Whatever the source of the rented time, the retail time buyer usually provides his own computer operator along with the program and the converted input data to be processed. This kind of computer time rental often imposes serious scheduling limitations on its user, but the machine time costs are likely to be lower than from any other source.

Some commercial banks and factors offer computer processing of selected accounting functions as part of their financial management service to their customers. In one case, a trucking company turned over its billing and accounts receivable processing to the bank that finances its operations. For a trucking company, the receivables function is complicated by the cross-billing from other carriers outside its own operational area who provide transportation for which the company bills its customers but for which the company must pay the other carriers. The bank processes this function to control the firm's financing operations, advancing funds to the trucking company against its net receivables rather than its billing. (In this particular case, the bank also handles accounts payable involving other carriers, thus further simplifying the trucking company's data processing operations.) A more restricted service is offered by some banks in billing and collection for doctors and dentists, using a data collection system like that described in Chapter 3 for ordering office supplies. In both cases, the user's on-premises support of the system involves little more than the data conversion and transmission functions. However, except in special circumstances, these processing services leave most of the user's data processing requirements untouched, thus reducing their value to company management. Another source of off-premises processing is exemplified by a regional stock exchange which offers complete transaction processing to its member firms. This kind of service is distinctly different from that offered by a bank, encompassing most, if not all, processing needed by the member firm, rather than a selected function. Groups of related companies (through a trade association, for example) have reversed this approach by setting up a captive computer center to perform their processing. The banking industry thinks so highly of this approach that it has sponsored legislation permitting banks to set up computer centers under jointly owned holding companies to service the owners' needs. Similarly, resort hotels in one area are investigating a joint reservations system like those used by the major airlines. Apart from collaborative actions (e.g., making alternative hotel reservations if the first choice is filled), a captive computer center offers facilities that no one user-owner could justify alone. Further, with data communications and time-sharing of the computer, each user has in effect independent access to the computer. Computer cooperatives of this type, with or without programming staffs, seem likely to proliferate in the next few years.

FINAL SYSTEM DESIGN

Final system design completes the specialization of the new system plan begun during approach selection, modifying the optimum system design to accommodate the facility chosen to implement it. Although the start of the final system design parallels that of facility selection and contributes to that process, the major effort awaits completion of the facility selection process. The parallel phase is similar to approach selection in that the optimum system design is adapted (either by the systems analyst or by the facility suppliers) to match the features each facility offers. These modified designs are then compared as one ingredient in the choice among the facilities being considered. After that choice is made, all design effort is devoted to realization of the new system with the chosen facility. For an on-premises computer facility, the parallel phase of final system design is particularly important for facility selection. For example, the design effort must divide batch processing operations into separate runs on the basis of input availability schedules, number and type of I/O devices, and computer storage capacity (which determines program length for a single run). In doing so, the design effort develops the I/O device and storage requirements to be met by the computer. In the same way, this parallel effort produces run time estimates and processing schedules (as discussed in Chapter 5) for each computer being considered. These estimates demonstrate whether a particular computer is adequate to handle the new system, with surplus capacity both for growth of the initial application and for additional applications. Similar considerations apply for a business equipment system in determining its adequacy (or, equivalently, the number of machines) to handle the system load.

Extensive use should be made of the support offered by the suppliers during this parallel phase of final system design. Each supplier should be asked to adapt the optimum system design for best results with the facility he recommends (unless the systems analyst has already shown that the facility will be inadequate). These recommendations are requested in support of facility selection, either as part of the formal proposals or in earlier informal presentations used to reduce the number of suppliers who will be asked to submit formal proposals. Supplier support should continue through the facility selection process and beyond. It assumes even greater importance to final system design after facility selection is completed. Although the successful supplier may offer to prepare the final system design for his portion of the new system, his offer is better taken initially for collaboration than for an independent effort. The systems analyst is concerned with the entire new system, not just the portion to be implemented by the supplier or his equipment. Accordingly, the supplier's offer to prepare the final system design for his portion of the over-all system should be kept in abeyance, except for suggestions, until the analyst has fully defined the integration requirements that portion must meet. Then, the task can be turned over to the supplier for execution under the supervision of the analyst, freeing the analyst to devote his major efforts to the rest of the system.

Final system design normally continues into conversion for and installation of the new system. However, management may well wish to review the results of final system design before this transition occurs and, more important, before a commitment is made to the new system. When this is the case, final system design should cut off for review after the new system procedures have been outlined in some detail but before detailed procedures (whether for manual or machine processing) have been developed. This cutoff point corresponds with the conclusion of facility selection, but precedes contracting for the implementing facility. For a computer system, the cutoff point is reached when the manual procedures to be used outside the computer proper have been defined and all problem definition data (described in Chapter 3) is ready for the start of the programming effort.

If the system is to be implemented by a computer center, the same cutoff point applies except that run definitions may be left to the computer center. However, record layouts and processing requirements must be defined just as precisely as for an on-premises system. For a business equipment system, the cutoff point is essentially the same, since most business equipment requires some programming in the form of control panel wiring. In short, final system design concludes when a complete blueprint of the new system has been developed and before construction from that blueprint is started.

8

FACILITY SELECTION

Facility selection for a new data processing system is complicated by the existence in the United States alone of over twenty computer manufacturers and more than ten business equipment makers (five of whom double in the computer field), all offering innumerable models for consideration. Add to this array the variety of off-premises computer facilities available throughout the country, to make the problem appear overwhelming. Fortunately, the problem of selection is less severe than it looks, for several reasons. For one thing, half of the computer manufacturers concentrate exclusively on the science-engineering market; their machines can be used for business data processing, but require more sophisticated programming than is customary for business applications. Another reason is that many of the proffered equipments will be ruled out as unsuitable, either by the new system requirements or by the equipment prices. Further, the range of choice is limited to the suppliers within reach of the prospective user. This question of proximity is particularly important in considering computer rental centers, even with the use of data communications, but also applies to maintenance support of on-premises equipment. Once the serious candidates are identified, factors such as programming assistance and training offered by each supplier come into play in evaluating the total worth of each candidate. The ultimate selection is based on these evaluations.

The selection process to be described in this chapter is specifically for choice of an on-premises computer, but it is also applicable, with some modifications, to selection of business equipment or the choice of an off-premises facility. The process does not differ much from procurement of any kind of major equipment. Once the need for new equipment is established and the requirements it must meet are determined, competitive bids are solicited from contending suppliers and are evaluated to select the equipment which best balances advantages against its costs. Facility selection starts from the optimum design for the new processing system to develop computer (or business equipment) system specifications that define the functional requirements to be met by the equipment. These specifications may be submitted to the contending suppliers for comments and suggestions, perhaps the best use of their support at this stage. When the specifications reach final form, they are turned over to the suppliers as the basis for formal proposals. The solicitation of these proposals also spells out the information to be provided in them. Proposal evaluation, with price as only one factor among many, then leads to selection of the equipment for the new system. These three elements of the selection process, namely, system specifications, proposal solicitation, and proposal evaluation, are important enough to deserve separate discussion.

SYSTEM SPECIFICATIONS

The specifications for a computer or business equipment system resemble the information derived from the feasibility study (discussed in Chapter 5) to obtain preliminary proposals. However, the system specifications cover only the automated portion of the new system, defining its processing requirements as completely as possible so that each supplier can determine which model and what features meet those needs most economically. An essential part of the system specifications is a system flow chart, which depicts the sequence of procedures to be performed by the automated portion, the frequency of their performance, and the logical file structure they demand. This logical file structure identifies functional requirements, not physical devices; a batch processing system may require five logical files without needing that many tape drive units. The statement of functional requirements is preferable to physical definitions because it frees the suppliers to investigate all reasonable approaches to implementation. For example, a supplier can now propose random access storage for a batch processing system if it offers significant advantages.

The system specifications must also contain information derived from the feasibility study but which is modified to reflect the new system. System files must be described in detail, including each file record layout, the number of records in each file, and the distribution of file activity (e.g., do 90 per cent of the transactions affect the same 10 per cent of the file records?). In the same way, input records are defined as to layout, volume by type, arrival schedules, and data flow rates (i.e., in a batch system, batch size and size variations). Similarly, output documents and reports must be fully described along with their production schedules. These figures on data volume must be supplemented by estimates of the growth in volume of each type of data over the useful life of the new system, usually three to five years.

The system flow chart for the new system identifies its procedures without spelling them out in detail. The suppliers need complete procedural descriptions to estimate their processing times and to determine the size of computer memory needed to hold their programs. The applicable descriptions and detailed flow charts developed for the optimum system design satisfy this requirement in the system specifications. The same information can be presented in more concise form as estimates of the number of COBOL (or FORTRAN) procedural statements necessary to code each procedure. These estimates, prepared by the systems analyst, greatly simplify the suppliers' projection tasks and also simplify proposal evaluation by putting the suppliers' projections on the same base.

If the new system is to accommodate other applications, the system specifications may need to reserve processing capacity for them. The scheduling requirements of the first application establish the minimum surplus capacity of the new system by indicating whether it will have any free days. Projected running times then show whether additional surplus capacity will be available on those days that the first application is being processed. The surplus capacity of the new system depends on the peak load requirements of the first application. If they are high, the system needs a larger or faster computer than otherwise, and so will have more surplus capacity. To determine the capacity needed for the other applications, some estimate must be made of their processing volume, scheduling requirements, and schedule of conversion to computer processing. If these applications require more capacity than is afforded by a system matched to the first application or if the composite scheduling requirements impose a high peak load on the system, the system specifications must reserve additional processing capacity. One way to reserve capacity is to specify that the first application be processed by the new system within some stated fraction of first-shift time on the computer.

The importance of capacity reservation is diminished somewhat by the compatibility of computers within each manufacturer's product line, which minimizes reprogramming for shifting to a larger computer in the same line. When a computer is rented, the manufacturer will normally allow a change to a larger computer before the expiration of the rental contract on the smaller machine. Yet the change-over can easily disrupt normal operations or, at best, require space to install and ready the new computer for operation before the old one is removed. When a computer is purchased, the user is committed to his machine for five years, and possibly longer, to achieve a payoff and to write off the computer's price completely. (As this is written, no "Blue Book" on used computers exists. Manufacturers' trade-in allowances have gone as high as one-quarter, but average closer to one-tenth of original purchase price.) If his sale depends on early delivery, the computer manufacturer may offer a smaller machine to serve in the interim, possibly on a rental basis with the fees applied to purchase of the later and larger machine. If so, the change-over is more dependent on the manufacturer's production schedule than on the user's growth in volume and range of applications, although good Yankee horse-trading may shift the balance. In short, capacity reservation is worthwhile for a rented or a purchased computer.

Capacity reservation invokes other considerations for "compatible" computers that are available in a graded set of models in each line, differing in size, speed, and cost. Each model is offered in a range of configurations that fits between or even overlaps the capabilities of its smaller and larger neighbors in the product line. The maximum configuration of a small model may provide greater processing capacity than the minimum configuration of its larger neighbor, yet leave no room for expansion. Since most first-time computer users have underestimated their processing needs, it follows that the largest justifiable model in its minimum configuration may be a better choice than a large configuration of the smaller model. This choice will result in a low utilization factor for the computer system, indicating that capacity is available for other applications. The low utilization factor is not important if the system is justified. Some applications have made profitable use of a computer that stands idle 90 per cent of the time. As an example, a demand processing system, which must operate at all times, is often implemented with two computers, each of which can handle the system peak load. One computer is always active in processing the demand operation and may intermix some batch operations. The other computer is on standby for the demand operation, taking over if the first computer fails and when the first computer is due for scheduled maintenance. The standby computer is also available for batch processing, but can easily be idle for most of the time available on it.

PROPOSAL SOLICITATION

Although system specifications are vital in soliciting proposals for a computer system, they cannot guarantee that the proposals will be responsive or easy to evaluate. To give that assurance, the proposal solicitation should spell out the information items to be provided in the proposals. These items are identified in the following outline and then discussed in some detail. The outline is indicative rather than exhaustive in that circumstances may require other elements in the proposals. For example, current equipment may be offered to determine its trade-in value or the user may require implementing facilities ahead of reasonable equipment delivery dates. These special circumstances are not treated in the following outline but, if they exist, should be detailed in the proposal solicitation along with the elements listed below.

The outline of information to be specified in the proposal solicitation is as follows:

A. *Hardware*
   1. Recommended equipment model and configuration in detail, including special (i.e., extra-cost) features
   2. Accessory equipment needed (e.g., key punches, magnetic tapes, disc packs, tape or disc pack dead storage equipment)
   3. Site preparation requirements
   4. Delivery and installation schedules

B. *Software*
   1. Availability of supervisor or operating system programs (if applicable), compilers, assemblers, conversion programs, and standard operation or utility programs, etc.
   2. Availability and applicability of existing programs for similar applications

C. *Personnel* (recommended staffing levels for)
   1. Equipment operation
   2. Data conversion and preparation
   3. Continued (as opposed to first-time) programming

D. *Performance Estimates*
   1. Projected run times and processing schedules for the application(s) in the specifications
   2. Calendar of surplus time, excluding scheduled maintenance
   3. Benchmark problem

E. *Expansibility*
   1. Processing capacity of the recommended configuration in comparison with that of the maximum configuration for this model
   2. Limitations or prerequisites for expansion of the recommended configuration

F. *Conversion Support*
   1. Personnel offered for first-time applications programming

2. Training for user personnel
3. Machine time, prior to installation, for file conversion and maintenance, program testing, general familiarization, etc.

G. *Costs and Terms of Rental or Purchase*
  1. Detailed costs by item for rental of the recommended configuration and estimates of costs for materials (e.g., punched cards, magnetic tapes, printer forms)
  2. Cost of purchase option with rental contract and period of rental
  3. Price for purchase of the recommended configuration and cost of supplementary maintenance agreement
  4. Compensation for equipment failure and backup services available in case of failure
  5. Availability of maintenance services and conditions on rental or on purchase

H. *Other Users*
  References to nearby users of compatible equipment for opinions on the supplier and for potential backup arrangements.

The information requested on hardware, software, and personnel needs little comment, with some exceptions. First, software comprises the standard programs and the program-writing programs that extend and may even determine the capabilities of the hardware to be procured. Second, the terms *delivery* and *installation* have special meanings in the world of computers. The delivery date is the date on which the hardware arrives at the user's premises. The installation date is the one on which the computer is turned over to the user in working order. Finally, the array of items mentioned under software is less important than the fact of their current existence or nonexistence. Too many "pioneers" have suffered from the nonexistence and late delivery of these software items to let the question pass without notice. The existence and estimate of applicability of programs for similar applications is comforting if not conclusive. This information element may well be coupled with the request for programming support from the supplier (see F.1 in the outline), to confirm the applicability estimate or to remove it from consideration if the supplier offers to adapt the existing programs without (explicit) cost to the user.

The performance estimates and expansibility information (requested in D and E of the outline) establish the adequacy of the proposed system for current and projected processing loads. The benchmark problem (D.3) refers to a timed run of standard data to evaluate the proposed hardware (and software, if compiling or assembly is required). A proposal can offer the running of a benchmark problem, but cannot give results unless the user has a machine-independent program (e.g., in COBOL) and includes it in the solicitation along with test data to be processed. Even then, a benchmark problem is normally run in the presence of the prospective user to allow his verification of the run timing. The item on limitations of expansibility (E.2) raises the possible problem of adding to a purchased machine when the manufacturer prefers not to do so. The intent here is to obtain a prior commitment to offer these additions if the purchaser requests them at a later date. (It may also be worthwhile to inquire about installation of manufacturer's improvements after purchase and their cost, if any, although no problem is likely to arise if the manufacturer is responsible for maintenance of the purchased equipment.)

Conversion support (F in the outline) is a crucial element of the proposals, since it strongly affects the first-time costs incurred by the prospective user. Programming support (F.1) and training (F.2) have obvious implications. Machine time (F.3) may seem equally obvious, although it has more far-reaching implications. As will be seen in Part III, file conversion is a major task in preparing for a computer system. Similarly, program testing is essential if the new system is to perform reliably as soon as it is put into use. Machine time is necessary for both tasks and must be available in sufficient quantity to accomplish both prior to installation of the new system. Some companies have been willing to "pioneer" on new machines, depending on the additional programming support offered by the manufacturer to offset the lack of machine time; their expectations were not always fulfilled, since added programming support is not equivalent to time on a computer.

Costs and terms information (G in the outline) should be self-evident except, perhaps, for items G.4 and G.5. A manufacturer's liability for equipment failure can depend upon whether the equipment is rented or purchased and, in the latter case, on whether the manufacturer provides maintenance. On rented equipment, the user is exempt from rental charges while the equipment is unavailable for use; most manufacturers will not assume any further obligation for nonperformance by their equipment. With purchased equipment, the manufacturer will normally offer no compensation for failure beyond that provided in the equipment warranty (or guarantee), regardless of whether he has contracted for its maintenance. An outside maintenance service for purchased equipment generally offers no compensation for equipment failures. However, a maintenance contract can include penalties for tardiness in responding to a maintenance call, where tardiness may be defined as a delay of more than 2 hours at one extreme or more than 24 hours at the other extreme. Item G.5 should elicit information about this definition of tardiness and also about the differences, if any, in maintenance contracts for rental or purchased equipment.

The best answer to equipment failure is the use of backup facilities; i.e., the transfer of processing to another machine. In general, a manufacturer offers only limited backup services to his clients, whether they rent or buy his equipment. However, other users of similar equipment (H in the outline) are often willing to enter into reciprocal backup agreements, including provisos to handle overflow loads not caused by equipment failures. The references to nearby users of similar equipment thus has a dual value. First and foremost, their experience with the prospective supplier adds a useful perspective for analysis of his proposal, verifying the degree to which he performed his contractual obligations. Second, and of almost equal importance, these nearby users form the nucleus of an association for backup facilities.

A final note is in order on the proposal solicitation concerning proposal due dates and the award date. The suppliers who are asked to propose on the new system should be allowed enough time to answer the solicitation with due care and thoroughness. Allowing a month for proposal preparation is not excessive. The time period should start running from the date on which the solicitations are presented to the prospective suppliers. A date should be set, about a week later, for a meeting of supplier representatives with the soliciting organization, to answer questions arising from the solicitation. In addition, the soliciting organization should designate one man as information source through the period following the meeting. Both the questions he receives and the answers he gives should be conveyed to all prospective suppliers as soon as possible after the questions are presented. The proposal solicitation should also specify the award date if this is at all possible. This date for concluding the proposal evaluation phase (to be described next) allows the prospective suppliers to quote realistic delivery and installation dates in their proposals. The award date may follow the proposal due date by from one to three months, depending upon the time required by the suppliers to prepare for running of the benchmark problem if it is not already programmed. The delay allowed for benchmark problem programming, if necessary, is one topic to be settled during the meeting with the suppliers' representatives, keeping in mind that the period allowed for proposal preparation can also be used for this programming effort.

A really confident sales team may place a tentative order for its recommended equipment configuration as soon as it decides on the recommendation. This tentative order may leave the sales team "on the hook" for the month or more until the decision date arrives, but it will also advance by the same period the delivery date offered in the proposal. In specifying a decision date, management does not commit itself to any of the proposed equipments, since it can still decide not to change the current system. However, the specified decision date bars procrastination and may reap some of the benefits mentioned.

PROPOSAL EVALUATION

The most systematic procedure for proposal evaluation requires comparative scoring of each proposal element (on a scale from o to 10, for example), and then combination of the element scores for each proposal in accordance with preassigned weighting or importance factors for each element, to arrive at an over-all score for each proposal. Although this procedure sounds as if it were completely objective, it cannot eliminate the necessary element of judgment, the element usually demanded from management. For example, the weighting factors needed to put low price and early delivery on the same measurement scale can come only from management judgments. Similarly, judgment is needed to produce comparative scores on any one proposal element. Each element is normally submitted to the man or committee best qualified to evaluate it. If that element is also submitted to another man or group for scoring, the two sets of scores cannot simply be averaged, since that would give more weight to the less qualified evaluations. Accordingly, management judgment is needed in assigning proposal elements for comparative scoring as well as in assignment of weighting factors for those scores. A little trust could well accompany the scoring assignments, in view of the evident dependence on their results.

Despite these harsh words, the systematic procedure just described is the best one for proposal evaluation if it is not used as a substitute for normal management judgment. The preliminary task of assigning weighting factors to the various proposal elements can be a tricky one unless the goals for the new system are kept in mind. Obviously, the system rental or purchase price is a major proposal element; yet a low price can be offset by other proposal elements. A good rule of thumb in assigning weighting factors is to reflect the contribution of the element to total costs of the system over its useful life. Thus, if first-time programming costs can contribute only one-fifth as much as rental costs to the total system costs, the weighting factor on first-time programming support should be only one-fifth of the weighting factor on rental price. An alternative approach simply converts each proposal element, if possible, into an equivalent cost, to obtain a total system cost for the proposal. In some cases, first-time equivalent costs are separated from continuing costs for more careful analysis. Unfortunately, some proposal elements are intangibles, which do not convert easily or reasonably into equivalent cost figures, leaving the problem of combining these element evaluations with the cost figures to arrive at a total evaluation of the proposal. For these intangible elements, management must assign weighting factors that reflect their importance to the achievement of system goals.

An example of an intangible element is the availability of maintenance and repair services. A proposal that offers response to a maintenance call within an hour will also quote a higher rental price (or maintenance contract on purchased equipment) than will a proposal offering 4-hour response. An equivalent cost for the longer maintenance response time can be developed from estimated costs of substitute processing or customer dissatisfaction caused by equipment failures, but it will be extremely low because of low equipment failure rate and duration. (One computer manufacturer showed that the total failure time on all configurations of one computer model in the New York City area for the year 1963 averaged about 3 per cent of the available time on these machines.) A weighting factor based on equivalent cost will therefore be lower than the maintenance element deserves. Management is thus left with the task of assessing the value of rapid maintenance response against the higher rental price it usually entails.

Other intangible elements are judged as acceptable or unacceptable rather than being weighed. Examples in this category include software availability (particularly item B.1) and availability of machine time (item F.3), although the amount of machine time offered is subject to comparative evaluation. The performance estimates (item D) called for in the proposals also fit into this category, with the results of the benchmark problem intended to confirm the accuracy of these estimates. Similarly, the system expansibility (item E) indicates whether or not the proposed equipment can accommodate the projected load on the system. It is tempting to apply comparative evaluation to these two elements, but the results may be misleading. Obviously, an adequate system that offers more surplus capacity and expansibility at the same price as another adequate system is the better choice if all other factors are equal. However, too high a weighting factor on these two elements can lead to selection of a larger and more expensive computer than is justified for the system. A better approach is to allow a plus value for the equipment offering the largest surplus capacity or expansibility, or both, and then consider this and other plus values only secondarily to the composite weighted scores of the proposals.

Another proposal element that is difficult to evaluate is the delivery and installation schedule. Most computer manufacturers quote delivery from six months to two years after receipt of a firm order. Early delivery of a computer to a first-time user is a mixed blessing, since it cuts short the preparation time devoted to programming, training, and file conversion. Conversely, late delivery postpones the realization of gains from the use of a computer, and may impose large interim processing costs, particularly for maintenance of converted files, if the supplier does not allow enough machine time for this processing. The length of the delivery schedule depends on the size of the computer being proposed and on the degree of completeness of its design. As a result, a large computer requires a longer lead time, as does a newer computer. It is worth noting the tactic of proposing a new and untried computer if the supplier is not in a good competitive position with his production line. A potential user is wise to be wary of the role of "pioneer" with a new computer design, since he will share the problems of the manufacturer in proving both the hardware and the software. The manufacturer offers more support to a "pioneer" than otherwise; yet the user is probably ahead if he chooses a proven equipment for which software is already available, rather than risking his application on new equipment.

Proposal evaluation need not be performed in a closed-room, sealed-bid atmosphere, although the normal requirements of fairness to the prospective suppliers should be observed. Suppliers should be invited to modify unacceptable elements of their proposals or to explain the advantages of their proposed approaches if these are not clearly put forth in their proposals. The suppliers will welcome the opportunity to negotiate on various elements of their proposals, notably in the area of conversion support. Often, the supplier's sales team will expand its offer of support if this seems likely to improve the prospects of making the sale. A caution should be observed in connection with these offers of increased support; they are worthless unless they are written into the formal proposal in one form or another. Too often, a salesman has offered some extra service or support element verbally in all good faith, and then has been shifted to another territory or has taken a position with another employer. To avoid the misunderstandings or disappointments arising from the manufacturer's refusal to honor verbal commitments by his salesmen, these offers should be recorded in correspondence (e.g., a letter to the salesman setting out the offer he has made verbally to confirm its details) and appended to the formal proposal and resulting contract.

With reference to the performance estimates in the proposals, it was once customary for the manufacturer to guarantee the performance rates of his equipment under penalty of reduced rental if the equipment failed to meet its guaranteed rates. Computer manufacturers are increasingly reluctant to offer guarantees of this kind, mostly from sad experience with poorly defined applications and procedures. One potential computer user, for example, submitted for the benchmark problem run a record type that was not described in the definition of the problem. Oversights of this kind can throw off the best performance estimates and prevent the achievement of predicted processing rates. In lieu of a guarantee of performance rates, the potential user can negotiate with the prospective suppliers to obtain an acceptance testing period on the selected equipment before it is put on rental or before purchase payment is made. Essentially, the user demands a trial period in advance of the installation date, reserving the right to reject the equipment without incurring any settlement costs. This right is usually allowed by the computer manufacturers, whether or not it is specified in the contract. The formal inclusion of this right can prevent later unpleasantness if the equipment proves to be unsatisfactory.

TO RENT OR TO BUY?

In evaluating the proposals on computer equipments, the potential user must examine carefully the question of renting or buying the equipment for his system, even though the answer is usually determined by the capital structure of his company. Actually, the question is not twofold but fourfold, in view of the used computers offered for rental or purchase from nonmanufacturers. This mention of used computers raises some questions of its own, questions that are relevant to the basic decision. To start with, a computer manufacturer seldom offers used computers for rental or purchase (except when long-term renters are invited to purchase the machines they have been renting). Manufacturers offer for rental only "new" equipment, whether just built or reconditioned after prior use; equipment ordered for purchase is invariably built to order, including rebuilt components only if the original specifications indicate their inclusion. When a user rents equipment from its manufacturer, he need not be concerned about the inclusion of rebuilt or reconditioned equipment, since the manufacturer is responsible for its maintenance. Obviously, the rental fee includes an allowance to cover maintenance costs, but the user need not distinguish this portion from the remainder of the rental charge.

Computer manufacturers also offer their equipment for purchase at a price that equals the rental charges accrued over forty to fifty months. This ratio of purchase to rental price does not tell the whole story, since the rental fee includes maintenance services whereas the total cost for a purchased computer must include the costs of a maintenance contract along with the purchase price. Maintenance contract charges may run as high as 4 per cent of the manufacturer's rental charge, although lower figures can be obtained from independent maintenance services if they are accessible. Most computer manufacturers do not encourage users to purchase their equipment. For example, unlike the automotive industry, computer manufacturers do not offer credit arrangements for equipment purchase, although sale-and-leaseback and other arrangements can be made with conventional credit sources. The manufacturers do not discriminate against equipment purchasers, but will offer to purchasers conversion and first-time programming support which is comparable to the support afforded renters.

The rent-or-buy decision is complicated by the availability of older computers for rental or purchase from nonmanufacturers. These computers were originally purchased by their users and have been sold when new equipment was procured, rather than being turned back to the manufacturer for a trade-in allowance. These older computers do not match the performance of current equipment, but their reduced performance is matched by their reduced cost. For example, the federal government finds a continuing demand for a small vacuum-tube computer, which was introduced at the end of 1954, because its current cost is low enough to justify its use on applications that are too small for newer and larger computers. Rental of an older computer from a nonmanufacturer may or may not include maintenance services, often at the discretion of the user rather than the supplier. However, the supplier will usually provide conversion support (e.g., first-time programming and machine time) comparable to that offered by a computer manufacturer.

Purchase of an older computer from a nonmanufacturer is not normally accompanied by any conversion support or by any offer of maintenance service. Of course an older computer will have many programs prepared for it, usually available from the manufacturer without cost, thus reducing the importance of conversion support. Maintenance service is often a stickier problem, particularly with very old (i.e., vacuum-tube type) computers, since replacement parts may not be available. One insurance company has found it worthwhile, however, to procure such a computer and to staff and stock up for its maintenance. The experience with this machine has induced them to look for another one to increase their processing capacity without an equivalent increase in maintenance costs. Most users are not willing to accept this kind of maintenance responsibility. Therefore, an older computer is useful only if maintenance service is available locally, which is much the same problem discussed in connection with proposal evaluation.

A major factor in the rent-or-buy decision is that a computer is not made obsolete by the marketing of a newer, faster, and cheaper machine. Rather, a computer is obsolete only if it does not have enough capacity to accommodate the volume and range of applications put onto it, or waiting to go on it. It is true that a faster and cheaper computer may offer lower unit costs for processing, but the savings it offers may be canceled by the cost of conversion to its use. Too many computer users have succumbed to the "newer, faster, and cheaper" siren song every time it is played, incurring change-over costs before the replaced system reached its payoff point, and so postponing further the crossover into profitability from computer usage. In the early period of computer application to business processing, the risk was much higher that the ordered computer would be outdated in the interval between the order and the installation. Currently, the innovation cycle runs five to seven years from first installation of a computer model to first installation of its successor (although announcement of the successor precedes its installation by one or two years). Accordingly, the rent-or-buy decision is not particularly affected by technical obsolescence, since the useful (or payoff) life of a system is comparable to the life of a computer model.

Ultimately, the rent-or-buy decision is made on the basis of economics, just as is the prior decision to use a computer. A regulated company such as a public utility may benefit from purchase of a computer since this increases the capital base on which its allowable rate of return is calculated. In this case, a used computer is inadvisable because its book value is lower than that for a new computer. For an unregulated company, the return on investment in a purchased computer is compared with the return from other possible investments and with the effect of straight expenses from computer rental. Other alternatives should also be considered, including rental with option to purchase and the variety of sale-and-leaseback terms from credit organizations. The company's accountant can be particularly helpful in making the decision, by projecting the effects of these alternatives on company liquidity, operating expenses, and profitability before and after taxes. A first-time computer user may prefer to rent his computer even if he can realize savings from its immediate purchase. The rental period allows him to accumulate operating experience and may save him from premature commitment to an inadequate system. However, when he rents with an option to purchase, he will purchase a machine at a lower price than a new one, although it will have a shorter remaining life. As always, management must evaluate the intangibles of the question, guided by the projected costs and savings of each alternative.

Additional light is cast on the rent-or-buy decision, with particular consideration of financing and taxation questions, in the appendix prepared by Jerome Gartner, LL.B. He has also contributed the next chapter of this book, devoted to the legal problems that arise when a business changes over to computer data processing.

9

LEGAL PROBLEMS OF
COMPUTER ACQUISITION

by Jerome Gartner, LL.B.

This chapter highlights some of the legal problems that stem from adoption of computer equipment for business data processing and suggests solutions. The common element raised by this chapter is that, by installing computer equipment, the company is changing historical relations—both internally and with all its customers, suppliers, and governmental agencies—and therefore must review from a legal standpoint the effects the changes will make on the company's contracts and relationships with third parties.

The initial problem arises in negotiating a contract that will effectively provide the user with the service he desires, at the most economical cost, and include protection against the extremely costly delays that may occur in installation. A related problem is the question of whether the computer should be rented or purchased. Recently enacted tax laws make it difficult to determine the true cost of equipment. (It has been said that the Indians received a good price for Manhattan when they sold it for $24 in 1626. If the money had been invested at 6 per cent compound interest, it would approximate today's assessed valuation of all Manhattan real estate.) In somewhat less dramatic fashion the government tax regulations may permit purchase with less dollar expenditures than rental. This question is covered in the appendix to this book.

The computer involves extensive shifts in record keeping and record keeping techniques. As a result, new problems of preventing error, fraud, and control of personnel arise. The company needs to review carefully its duties as a record-keeping agent of governmental agencies, and its need for records to substantiate at a later date its transactions and methods of doing business. Management also needs to consider the effect of the computer on its labor relations.

One of the major pitfalls of using a computer is that heavy reliance must be placed on outside technical specialists who do not have an over-all or long-range view of the company's needs. Management cannot afford to rely solely on outside parties for the full understanding of their own business that is required for an effective computer system. Outsiders lack the requisite knowledge of the company's business or personnel and the ability to evaluate the degree of trust the company wants to place in each employee.

Management—including the accounting, auditing, tax, and legal staff—needs to acquire sufficient knowledge of how the computer system will function, before it can make effective use of outside advice and evaluate the proposals presented to it. The company's own legal and accounting personnel will be of little use in preventing future mistakes by the computer system unless the company consults them at the very start of the decision to install computers. Management must also see that they receive sufficient education in the mechanics of computer operation, so that they can offer knowledgeable advice to management.

CONTRACT PROVISIONS

The computer industry operates under a price umbrella established by IBM. There are no present indications that IBM is giving outright price discounts from their announced rental and purchase schedules. Some competition is more liberal, although the entire computer industry has tried to avoid direct discounts from list prices. The widest area for negotiation comprises extra services. In this area, all manufacturers (including IBM) have shown flexibility by including items that otherwise might be charged to the user, as part of the announced rental or purchase price. Many items are not in the manufacturers' printed contracts, but have been included successfully by users in their written contracts. This chapter discusses some of these items from the legal viewpoint.

A major purchaser of computer equipment will obtain greater concessions from the manufacturer, while a small user may find it impossible to modify in any significant way the manufacturers' contract. The points mentioned here represent expenses or risk of expenses that are present in all computer systems and which, if not borne by the manufacturer, will be paid by the user. It may be advisable to select a manufacturer whose equipment might otherwise not be first choice because of the greater nonequipment support that he will include as contract provisos.

Maintenance contracts are becoming increasingly more important as the economic life of computer equipment lengthens. NCR, who specializes in bank equipment, has a policy of providing service, including parts and labor, at a fixed price for periods ranging up to nine years and eleven months. This position had been strengthened by present General Services Administration regulations for federal purchases of computers requiring maintenance contracts for between seven and ten years, at a predetermined price.

Most computer manufacturers, if requested, will provide long-term maintenance contracts, including parts and labor, at a fixed price. Manufacturers will offer a warranty on the main frame and a partial guarantee on peripheral equipment. This difference is irrelevant when the company obtains a total parts and labor maintenance contract.

As an adjunct to the total parts and labor contract, a user should try to obtain a contract provision from the manufacturer that covers costs of down time on the equipment. The down time provision, if possible, should be broadly drafted to cover the costs the company will incur if a part of the computer system is down.

Where data are kept on magnetic tapes, loss of one of the tape drives may be sufficient to incapacitate the entire system and require all work to be done by a service bureau or other source of backup service until the tape drive is fixed. A good maintenance contract, from the user's view, would provide that the manufacturer absorb the costs resulting from the total down time, although the costs may exceed the rental or payments on that particular piece of equipment.

Software and Conversion

One of the major and often unrealized costs of computer installation is the software, or programs necessary for the desired applications. One computer consultant has estimated that software costs are equal to 15 to 18 months rental charges. It has been the practice of the manufacturers, and certainly of their salesmen, to offer to provide some of the necessary programs. A user would be remiss not to have spelled out in the contract, in as detailed form as possible, what the salesman has promised, including whether the manufacturer is responsible not only for providing the programs but also for making them operate successfully.

Changing computers, even by the same manufacturer, creates software problems, and programming may be as complicated for conversion from one computer to another as from manual operation to computer.

A good framework would be to obtain written commitments from the manufacturer of applications needed. Often the manufacturer's stock applications (payroll, etc.) will not be directly suited to the particular user's application. If so, an attempt to write a contract provision may clarify the manufacturer's position and the user's needs more precisely. Request for such a contract provision may result in the manufacturer's admitting that his stock applications will not satisfy the user's needs without considerable and costly modification. For example, consider payroll processing. The manufacturer could guarantee that the payroll system installed would effectively and efficiently, in dollar cost and computer time, do the job required.

The best insurance is that payments do not start until all applications specified in the contract are functioning properly, as opposed to the standard contract provision for rental or purchase payments to start when the equipment is properly installed.

Miscellaneous Provisions

IBM, if requested, has provided support personnel for six months after installation of a 1401-type computer. For comparable machines, the contract could and should specify such help. The availability of an experienced manufacturer's employee can be particularly valuable during the early period of computer operation.

Since time may be of the essence in starting computer operation, the manufacturer should be requested to provide off-premises computer capacity when the original delivery date is delayed because of problems that prevent putting the required applications into effective operation.

The usual maintenance contract calls for the user to provide adequate access to the computer equipment and storage space. If the computer installation is to be made in a high-cost area like midtown Manhattan, the contract should be more specific about space requirements, and the maintenance contractor should approve the plans in advance.

RECORD KEEPING

Introduction of a computer eliminates many procedures that have arisen over the last generation of the company's bookkeeping operation. The change-over will affect personnel as well as methods, but it will not alter the basic function of any accounting system—the effective control of money.

With the revolution in bookkeeping comes two major areas of trouble; new personnel and different opportunities for error and fraud. One virtue of a manual system that is lost by computer installation is the shift in responsibility from personnel tested by long years of honest and effective service. Some of the chances for error and fraud come out of the mechanical way in which entries are now handled, which excludes the previous safeguards of visual review by supervisory staff.

Examples of the changes involved in payroll accounting are presented below. The principles apply equally, however, to accounts receivable, accounts payable, and effective inventory control.

Payroll accounting in a computer installation can be mechanically handled, including the printing and mailing of the checks. The record prepared for each employee includes his gross salary, state and federal withholding taxes, social security contribution, and also deductions for savings bonds, life insurance, and purchases of company stock. A master file contains the record for each employee. Thereafter, in the usual course of business, new information is furnished to a clerk who prepares the changes for the master file.

Possibilities of error and fraud exist at each stage of the process of preparation. For example, manipulation may occur in the addition of names and new information furnished to the clerk who prepares the master file records or makes changes in them; or salary figures may be overstated; or checks of employees who have left may be continued.

These problems exist whether or not the company has a computer, but at the time of change-over, the personnel and quality of the employees handling payroll also change. With the shift to new personnel, who have not been tested by time and honest service, it is more necessary to institute careful controls. Such controls start with editing by a trusted employee of the data before it enters the system, using a procedure to verify amounts and employees on the payroll.

Control, after the initial information is verified, is substantially different from manual methods. A careful computer installation includes separation of the personnel who insert the new data on cards or magnetic tape from the computer room. Lack of access by the same person to both preparation of input data and running of the computer helps prevent fraud. A computer record is kept on magnetic tape or IBM cards. This offers the supervisor no visual record of the previous week's entries, such as provided by daily journals. The inability to supervise visually the preparation of input records is more reason to enforce rigidly the separation of computer personnel.

In a manual payroll system, only one person may be authorized to handle payroll checks. In a computer installation, a console operator, or anybody who operates the console, has the opportunity to write unauthorized checks. For this reason, programmers also should be physically separated from the console operations.

The last chance to catch mistakes is the print-out stage, where one control technique totals the checks printed and compares that total with the previously determined payroll total.

The war between cops and robbers is never-ending, and computers bring the problem into the electronic age. A financial institution discovered recently a fraud by an employee who was siphoning off for deposit into his own account a sizable sum of money each quarter-year. The funds came from lack of a provision in programming for breakage, similar to race-track breakage, which happened when the bank rounded the interest off to three places. The $4\frac{1}{3}$ per cent interest per annum was a repeating decimal (1.083333) input, and when the amount of this decimal to three places was multiplied, fractions of a penny were left over in the calculation of each account. The employee satisfied the accounting control on the total interest deposited each quarter by putting the breakage in accounts in his own name in the bank. The amount lost from each account was only fractions of a penny or pennies, but the breakage from several hundred thousand accounts was substantial. This theft occurred because, with the computer equipment, one man was capable of handling posting of interest, which had been handled previously by a number of bookkeepers.

Although management needs to take adequate steps to protect against fraud and error, the advantages of the computer are lost if the controls are too cumbersome. If four or five people review checks, there is less chance of loss, but the cost will absorb the savings. As a result, some companies have established guide lines for areas of greater risk, i.e., payments under $100 may be made without extensive supervision. Moreover, it may be more damaging to have a customer billed twice than have a small false pay check cashed.

Similar problems of safety apply to all areas of accounting.

RECORD RETENTION

Modern business is the unpaid agent for many government agencies for the collection of taxes and the maintenance of many government records like Social Security. Shifting to key punch cards and to magnetic-tape records substantially changes the form in which these records will be maintained. In many cases, the company has the stated or implied burden to see that the necessary records are maintained.

One example is the duty of each company to conform to the requirements of state and federal Fair Labor Standards Acts. The laws set forth both minimum wages and (in some cases) additional wages to be paid for overtime, night, and week-end work, as well as specified number and time of hours to be worked by categories of labor (i.e., women). In a noncomputer system, time cards are the usual evidence of the number of hours and time of day the employee is worked. Sophisticated data collection systems are now in use for multiplant companies where time cards are replaced by the reading of employee badges. These badges are inserted in data communication terminals, which transmit the information directly to the home office computer from the various plant locations in a random fashion (i.e., all employees punching in between 8:49:00 and 8:49:10). This information is stored on punched cards and magnetic tape, which is sorted weekly on the computer to prepare payroll checks. The original cards or magnetic tapes may not be saved for more than one accounting period, the information being added to an updated master tape.

Use of a cumulative master tape means that time records for a particular weekly or monthly period will not be available several years later if questions arise concerning a particular employee's work records or overtime, which may be related to a state or the federal Fair Labor Standards Act. In deciding questions based on fact arising several years earlier, most courts give great weight to contemporaneous written records made in the ordinary course of business. Time cards are just such records. Lack of time cards may have the practical effect of shifting to the employer the burden of proving why the employee's testimony should not be believed. And the employer will have the added handicap that the courts are not yet familiar with record keeping by computer. A solution to this problem and others like it is the added weekly print-out. Where badges are used, the print-out of checks could be supplemented by an additional sheet, which would show the time and number of hours worked by the employee and which would be signed by him when he receives his pay check.

It is not possible to determine precisely which records may be needed several years later. However, before any record form with significant value as evidence is discarded as the result of computer installation, it should be carefully reviewed.

LABOR RELATIONS

One serious side effect of computer installations is that relating to employee relations and union contracts. The most costly strikes in recent years have been over the installation of automated equipment. The *New York Post* was briefly struck in 1965 over the issue of using a computer to replace linotypists.

A computer needs new personnel skills and may require dislocation of existing employees. Certainly, as careful planning should be done for the employee shifts as for the accounting procedure changes. The usual two-year gap between start of negotiations and delivery of computer equipment provides time for the necessary adjustments. In many cases, existing personnel can be retained for the new jobs in computer operation. The manufacturers have set up extensive school facilities for this purpose. The Metropolitan Life Insurance Company has found that bright high-school graduates can be successfully trained as programmers.

Existing labor contracts often do not adequately provide for computer installation and possible job dislocation. Management and labor benefit by raising these questions as early as possible. One of the major causes of the lengthy shipping strike of 1965 was management's failure to discuss with the union the manning of the automated ships, which the union knew were under construction.

The usual experience has been that computer installation does not result in loss of jobs. Management's savings come in the reduced personnel requirements as the work load increases in future years. Some sophisticated computer installations do result in a centralization of accounting personnel in the home office. A computer installation, therefore, may require review of the company's union contracts in locations other than the site of the computer.

PART IV

SYSTEM INSTALLATION
AND OPERATION

When management decides to adopt the new business data processing system that results from the feasibility study and system design efforts, preparations for the new system must be started immediately if they are to be completed by the time the new equipment is delivered. These preparations, mostly first-time conversion and training tasks, require careful planning and adequate staffing to meet the deadline and to assure successful operation of the new system. The supplier normally provides vital support for these preparatory tasks, but his support will taper off when the new equipment is put into operation. The user is ultimately responsible for continued operation of the new system, and therefore must plan and carry out his preparations, with assistance from the equipment supplier, to achieve that goal.

This fourth part of the book discusses the preparation for installing and operating an on-premises computer system, and is applicable to any new processing system with only slight modification. The tasks involved are grouped under three headings, indicated below, with each group covered in a separate chapter:

1. Planning of and preparations for installation of the new system (Chapter 10)
2. Conversion of processing operations onto the new system, in-

cluding establishment of new manual procedures for the new system (Chapter 11)

3. Monitoring of new system operation to maintain its responsiveness to management goals through improvements and added applications (Chapter 12)

The preparatory phase is essentially a continuation of final system design, involving personnel selection and training, applications programming, master files conversion, and physical site preparation for the new system equipment. Completion of this phase is normally synchronized with the new equipment delivery date, thus requiring careful planning of this phase and of the next one for successful change-over to the new system.

After the new equipment is delivered and the preparatory phase is completed, the actual change-over to the new processing system begins. In this phase, the new equipment must be tested for acceptability before it is turned over to the user. A separate series of tests is needed to validate each of the application programs before the complete processing system is tested. This processing system test, or shakedown operation, includes the manual procedures that are performed outside the computer proper, thereby confirming over-all system operation. Once this system shakedown is completed successfully, the new system must handle all processing for the applications put onto it.

The new processing system cannot be taken for granted after it becomes operational. The system embodies the best evaluation of company processing needs as of the time those needs were studied. These needs change as the using company grows and changes, demanding flexibility in the processing system to change accordingly. In particular, management must demand responsiveness to its ever-changing information needs and goals, overriding the inertia of processing system personnel.

10

PREPARATION FOR
THE NEW SYSTEM

The preparations for a new processing system build the structure laid out in the blueprint produced by system design. These preparatory tasks are heavily supported by the equipment manufacturer, but still demand considerable effort from the user organization. The largest task is that of selecting the operating and supporting staff for the new system, as well as the training of that staff and other affected company personnel. Next in size is the task of programming each application to be processed by the new system, along with development of the manual procedures for operations performed outside the processing equipment. Of comparable size is the task of compiling, refining, and converting master files for each application to be processed, together with the maintenance (i.e., keeping up to date) of these files pending operation of the new system. Finally, the equipment site must be prepared physically, and operating supplies must be procured.

All preparatory tasks mentioned above must be completed by the time the equipment is delivered if it is not to sit idle. Performance of these tasks can easily take up the full interval between the ordering of a computer and its delivery. In fact, the proposed delivery date is often postponed by the user, to allow more time for his preparations. Sufficient time and manpower must be allocated to these preparatory tasks, since they directly determine the effectiveness of the new system. In addition, time should be allowed for the learning process through which the user organization goes during this preparatory phase.

PLANNING AND PROGRESS CONTROL

The built-in deadline for the preparatory phase and the costliness of the change-over period force careful scheduling and continuous monitoring to allow corrections of schedule deviations as soon as they are detected. The preparatory phase schedule is usually developed in the form of a "countdown," working backward from the equipment delivery date to the present. However, the allocation of time to different tasks must account for their interrelationships. For example, programmer training must be completed before the programming effort gets under way, and so on. In general, the time allowed for a task determines the manpower assigned to it, with the caution that doubling the manpower does not halve the time required for completion of the task.

The most useful approach to scheduling and manpower allocation for the preparatory phase uses the critical path method (abbreviated CPM) in conjunction with PERT (Program Evaluation and Review Techniques). Although these techniques are covered thoroughly in existing publications, a brief description may be useful here.

PERT, in its simplest terms, considers a project as made up of subprojects, each with its own scheduled completion date. The term *milestone* is used to describe each of these subproject or task completion dates, and progress is measured by the approach to each milestone. This description is, of course, trivial in these terms; however, PERT goes beyond this trivial level to systematize the projection of expected progress and the evaluation of actual progress against these projections, to maintain the over-all project schedule.

The critical path method (CPM), an essential tool for PERT, can be described more explicitly by explaining its name. A critical path of a project is that string of interdependent tasks which takes the most time from start of the first through completion of the last. These tasks form a string, or path, because each one cannot be started until the preceding one is completed. To determine the critical path through a project, a CPM chart is prepared, depicting each project task as a line on what looks like a road map (or spider's web). Each line begins at the termination point of all directly prerequisite task lines, and so on. Incidentally, these termination points or groups of them are usually chosen as the PERT "milestones" for progress evaluation. After all tasks have been mapped onto this CPM chart and appended with execution time estimates, the critical path is found by determining the "longest" (i.e., most time consuming) path through the project. If the critical path fits within the time allotted for the project, the manpower loading on which the estimates were based is satisfactory; if not, manpower loading for the tasks in the critical path must be shifted to shorten that path. Of course this process may make another path the critical one, but the juggling can continue until either a satisfactory loading plan and schedule is obtained or the over-all schedule is proved to be too short to complete the project with the personnel and facilities available for it.

The CPM chart is useful in maintaining progress and in determining corrective action for schedule slippages as well as in drawing up the initial schedule for the project. Obviously, a lagging task on the critical path affects the over-all schedule, and must be corrected if the schedule is to be maintained. On the other hand, lags on a noncritical path can be tolerated to the point at which that path becomes the critical one. Thus, the CPM chart identifies the priorities to be accorded to slippage make-ups and the tolerance of accumulated slippage in each noncritical path. A caution to be observed is that the CPM chart is no better than the task time estimates on which it is based. If an early task took longer than its estimate allowed, the estimates for similar tasks should be extended unless a "learning curve" response is expected; i.e., the personnel have learned from the first task and can go on to perform the subsequent tasks in less time.

A final note on progress control concerns the frequency of progress reporting. It should be apparent that a report on the due date of, "We didn't make it!" is less useful than a report halfway to the due date of, "We're not going to make it!" At least some corrective action can be taken on the latter report. Carrying this argument to the extreme would lead to daily progress reports, whereas this frequency is too high to be justified. Weekly progress reports seem to satisfy most needs, pointing up slippages before they grow too large, without imposing an intolerable burden on the personnel who file the reports. Again, the accuracy of these reports is crucial to progress monitoring; the personnel who file them must be convinced that a report of schedule slippage is an appeal for help rather than a form of self-incrimination.

STAFFING AND TRAINING

Staffing for a new processing system begins with the choice of a data processing manager. That title can apply to anyone from a top-level executive who administers a large in-company service group down to a production supervisor for data conversion and computer operation personnel. (At this middle-management level, the supervisor is likely to report to someone in company management who exercises the true data processing control in addition to his other duties; but see the discussion in Chapter 3.) The first task facing the data processing manager is the planning and scheduling of the preparatory phase described above. The next task is that of selecting and training the personnel who will execute the preparatory phase tasks and the personnel for subsequent system operation.

In general, the staffing for the preparatory phase is not the same as the staffing for system operation. For example, programming manpower (or womanpower) requirements are much higher during the preparatory phase than during operation, although this peak loading is offset in whole or in part by the equipment manufacturer's programming personnel. Conversely, computer operators are not needed until the computer is delivered, but they must be chosen and trained during the preparatory phase. The requirements for clerical help and for machine operators (e.g., key punch operators) during the preparatory phase depend on the scheduling of master file conversion. This conversion task can be scheduled over a long enough period for execution by a clerical staff of operating size. However, a stretch-out of the conversion task complicates the maintenance of these files, since updating usually cannot start until the conversion is completed. In all these areas, manpower estimates by the equipment manufacturer are extremely useful, based as they are on experience with similar installations.

The question obviously arises as to how to select personnel for the new system staff, beginning with the manager. As described in Chapter 3, the manager must deal with and evaluate the performance of technical people (e.g., programmers) as well as schedule and administer the clerical and machine operations that keep the system running. If the new system is large enough, it is advisable to hire an experienced data processing manager or someone with closely related experience (e.g., shift supervisor at a large installation). If the system is too small to justify an administrator, someone in the company management (preferably in a staff rather than line position) should be trained for these duties, with the assistance of the equipment supplier. For an intermediate system, an intermediate solution is required.

In choosing analysts and programmers, a decision must be made between hiring experienced personnel and training your own. Experienced programmers are available in or near large cities and often in college communities. Their salaries are higher than those for trainees, but they require little or no investment in training (e.g., salaries while the trainees attend programming school). An experienced programmer is more valuable if his experience has been gained on the computer line or with the programming language (e.g., COBOL) being used in the new system; other experience is transferable but less valuable. Conversely, an experienced programmer is unlikely to know anything about the business in which your company is engaged, so some learning is required even in this case.

Training your own programmers may be a better choice, particularly to retain current employees whose positions will be abolished or curtailed by the new system. Their retention may be mandatory by labor agreement, or their experience may be of value to the company, or such training may be desirable to avoid resentment (and even sabotage) of the new system. The same considerations apply, of course, to the retraining of current clerical personnel.

Most computer manufacturers offer an aptitude test to select the candidates for programming school from among current employees. This test emphasizes general intelligence or reasoning ability and, surprisingly, spatial relations; i.e., the ability to perceive patterns and shapes. Whatever the test used, an employee who is bright and fairly flexible in his thought patterns stands a good chance of making a good programmer. The programming courses offered by the computer manufacturer are generally free of charge to the prospective user, as are the key punch and computer operator courses. In this case, the only expenses incurred are the employees' salaries (and possibly maintenance expenses, if away from home) and the costs of replacement labor during their absence from their regular duties. Even if a programmer candidate fails to complete the course, his partial training is useful for other jobs in the system. The retrained employees who finish the programming course will be nursed through their initial programming efforts by the experienced programmers on loan from the computer manufacturer during the preparatory phase. These loaned programmers will act as mentors to the neophytes, assisting them in producing actual programs until they can confidently proceed alone.

Many companies have been tempted by the prospect of hiring only programmer trainees because of their low salaries. This temptation ignores the investment in training and the risk of losing that investment if the trainee moves to another job before the cost of training is recouped. The banking industry, with its traditionally low salary scale (although offset by fringe benefits), has been forced into this practice. However with annual personnel turnover in their programming staffs approaching 60 per cent, many banks have re-examined this approach. The problem is so acute that banks in larger cities will not hire programming trainees because the salary advancement rate from that start is too slow to meet competition. Instead, they hire junior programmers (i.e., personnel trained in programming who have limited experience in the field) at higher starting salaries and with prospects of faster salary increases.

The training of computer operators is often neglected, even though the manufacturer offers a course without charge. The alternative of on-the-job training can be effective, but it ignores the importance of the operator to computer efficiency, particularly for batch processing applications. An unskilled operator may take as long to set up and tear down a batch processsing run as is taken for the run itself, thus doubling the effective processing costs for that run. An unskilled operator may be unable to correct an error condition that stops a processing run, forcing a later rerun from the start after other personnel have straightened out the problem. Still worse, an operator can easily destroy a master file inadvertently, requiring costly and time-consuming recovery procedures to reconstruct the lost master file, before normal processing can be resumed. Finally, an operator who is poorly trained or motivated may skip the control procedures that protect the computer user against fraud. The manufacturer's training courses cannot per se prevent these problems. The formal training in this course should, however, minimize them, and in contributing to the operators' sense of importance should motivate better performance of their duties.

Often equally neglected are the personnel who control the master file and program libraries, particularly for a magnetic-tape system but of comparable importance for systems using disc packs or magnetic-card magazines. This segment of the computer system staff needs little training about the computer itself, since their duties are essentially those of librarians. The items they control have low intrinsic value ($50 to $250 each), but the information carried on these items may be literally priceless. A careless librarian may issue a master file tape as a scratch tape (i.e., one that can be written on) and so destroy the master file as effectively as could be done by an operator error. Again, a careless librarian may innocently contribute to fraudulent schemes by failing to keep the issue and return records on programs and master files. These records, together with the operator logs, constitute the major controls of computer operation security. (Demand processing depends more on the integrity of the personnel who originate input data and on reasonableness checks in the programs.) It follows that the training of librarians is less important than their motivation and sense of responsibility, qualities that may be enhanced by the prestige of a formal training course.

PROGRAM DEVELOPMENT

The initial programming effort for a computer system is likely to be the most expensive task of the preparatory phase. The manufacturer absorbs some of the expense by lending experienced programmers without charge to the user. Yet, even with this contribution, the user's costs are likely to be as much as the first-year rental costs for the system equipment. Part of this cost is attributable to the short conversion timetable, usually further shortened by the training course for new programmers. Lack of time requires additional programming manpower, whether on or off premises, and imposes added costs accordingly. Another part of this cost is due to the inexperience of newly trained programmers, although this is minimized by the experienced programmers on loan from the manufacturer. The largest element of programming costs may stem from changes to the system design and the problem definitions they have produced. Some of these changes arise from management's greater appreciation of the system capabilities as the programming effort proceeds, but other changes are the result of inadequate management review during the system design phase. Management would do well to review the new system "blueprint" again while the programmers are being trained, to reduce the number of costly structural changes made after the programming effort has started. (See Chapter 7.)

The programming effort should be supervised by the systems analyst who prepared the system design it is implementing. He can pass on modifications suggested by the programmers (as discussed in Chapter 3), since he can determine their effects on the rest of the system. If management decides to have some of the initial programming effort handled by a computer center, the analyst may recommend that the packages be prepared outside. He acts as liaison and quality control on these outside efforts just as he does for the on-premises programming work.

One of the most important supervisory tasks is the monitoring of adherence to programming standards and documentation requirements by the programmers. Programming standards prescribe certain programming practices that keep programs compatible, make their use easy for the computer operators, and allow programmers other than the originators to work on them. For example, the programming standards may specify the use of COBOL EXTENDED '61-'67 (or FORTRAN or PL/I and more recent versions) for all programs unless the data processing manager authorizes the use of another language. The programming standards must specify the utility (i.e., standard operation) programs available to the system and insist that they be used to forestall wasteful reprogramming of these operations. The computer operators' lives are simplified if the programming standards set up mandatory error indications for common error conditions. These standard indications are more readily recognized by the operators than is the programmers's home telephone number or other such esoteric notices. By way of explanation, some computers indicate an error that prevents further processing by halting with a particular storage address displayed; this halt address indicates the type of error. Other computers provide a diagnostic message to identify the error and go on automatically to the next processing run on the schedule. In either case, standard indications ease the operators' tasks considerably.

Programming standards cover a much larger field than has been indicated so far. The computer manufacturer can offer valuable assistance in surveying that field and proposing standards for adoption by the user. If these standards are adopted before the programming staff is chosen, their objections are likely to be milder in tone than if the programmers are allowed to operate without standards. In the long run, programmers grudgingly approve of standards because of the arbitrary choice they make among bewildering alternatives, and because of the context they provide for the programmers' own tasks.

Programming documentation is one of the standards areas that is most bitterly opposed by programmers; yet it serves at least three purposes of interest to them, as follows:

1. Adequate documentation allows the systems analyst to review the programmer's initial efforts before he has wasted too much time "barking up the wrong tree."

2. Documentation assists the programmer in testing and proving

out his program and relieves him of the task of training the computer operators to run his program.

3. Documentation enables the programmer (or another programmer) to return to a completed program after six weeks, six months, or a year and make changes without having to recode the original program to discover what it is doing.

The first purpose is served when the programmer develops flow charts for review by the analyst before he starts coding. Many programmers dislike this task, preferring to plunge directly into coding from the analyst's problem definition. They argue that these preliminary flow charts will differ considerably from the coding that follows them, in time if not in structure, requiring complete revision of the flow charts after the coding has "jelled." This argument is comparable to the approach of a seasoned speaker who prefers not to prepare an outline of his speech before he gives it. The argument is valid, however, only if the problem definition supplied by the analyst is quite detailed. Otherwise, the analyst should insist on (and the programming standards demand) detailed flow charts from the programmer prior to the start of coding.

Final flow charts are essential to the programmer for his job of testing out his program. They serve as road maps to his detailed coding, allowing him to localize within specific segments of his coding the problems uncovered during program testing. Similarly, comments within the body of his coding and blocking of his coded program into separable elements assist him during program test and help him or another programmer to incorporate later program changes. Finally, the programmer's preparation of an instruction manual for the computer operators forces him to review the operating features of his program, quite apart from freeing him of the job of training the operators to run his program.

During the initial programming effort, a rather bothersome problem must be resolved, namely, that of handling exceptional transactions within each application. These exceptional items normally represent only a small fraction of the total transaction volume, and differ enough from other transaction types to require special program routines. If all exceptional items were to be handled by the computer, the program for the processing run might easily become too large to fit within the computer's memory, thereby jeopardizing efficiency for high-volume items. Decisions on the handling of exceptional items should be deferred until the programmers have investigated the subject. Items that appear to be exceptional may be amenable to processing by a combination of steps from the routines for several different transaction types, thus allowing their processing by the computer with little increase in memory space. Those exceptional items that do not succumb to this approach may still be processed part way into the system with no serious penalty of memory space for the program. In the latter case, the computer system should carry processing as far as is practical, and then turn out the item for manual continuation and call for confirmation that the manual processing has been done.

A related problem is the handling of transactions that contain errors or omissions. A demand processing system deals with this case by rejecting the entry and requiring its resubmission correctly and completely. In a batch processing system, this summary rejection is not usually the best solution. Batch processing runs so much faster than is humanly possible (in contrast to demand processing, which is designed to match human speeds) that a rejected transaction cannot re-enter the system before the processing run is completed, delaying its processing until the next, similar batch arrives. To avoid this kind of delay, the processing programs should be designed to work around errors or omissions in the transactions submitted to them, if this is at all possible. For example, if an employee's weekly time record fails to account for a working day, the payroll processing run might better charge him for a day of personal leave or vacation (if he is entitled to either of these charges) and put out his pay check in the normal sequence, rather than reject the problem for outside resolution and delay preparation of the employee's pay check. After all, the omission can be corrected during the next payroll period, particularly if the employee is notified of the problem and the temporary resolution. He is likely to want to reclaim that day of vacation or personal leave.

Other problems of errors or omissions may be less easy to circumvent, but the basic principle is the same. A sales order that fails to specify the color (or some other variable) for one item out of four should be processed through the three defined items and as far as possible toward the fourth item, to the extent perhaps of choosing a popular substitute. Of course, in this case, the system must request the omitted specification by printing out an error-handling report and must indicate the action it has taken on the correspondence (e.g., bill of lading) to the customer. As in the case of exception handling outside the computer, the program should include provisions for outside follow-up and report-back on disposition of the item. The computer is thus used as an ultrareliable control to prevent exceptional items from getting lost in the system, whether they are exceptional in and of themselves or made so by errors or omissions.

The entire program preparation phase is dependent on the availability of time on a computer like the one ordered for the new system, both for preparation of the programs in executable form and for testing of these programs. If the programs are written in a machine-independent language such as COBOL EXTENDED '61-'67, FORTRAN, or PL/I and subsequent versions, they must be submitted to a computer for compilation into symbolic language form and subsequent assembly from that form into object or machine language. Programs written in symbolic language can bypass the compilation process, but must still be assembled before they can be run for testing. The compilation and assembly processes usually turn up programmer errors in the use of the language, but not errors in processing logic because these are beyond the power of the compiler or assembler. These language-error finds often lead to logic corrections by the programmers, but the object programs can be proved out only by running them with representative test data on a computer that matches the one to be used in the new system. The computer manufacturer makes machine time available to prospective users for program testing and for familiarization with machine operation. Since this time is usually limited, the user programming staff must prepare well and carefully to get full value from the time allowed for program testing. The computer manufacturer can offer valuable advice about this preparation, since it is to his interest to achieve effective program testing within the machine time he can allot to the customer.

PROGRAM TESTS

First and foremost on the list of preparations for program testing is the desk checking of each program, preferably by another programmer. Desk checking is just what the name implies: sitting at a desk with the program before you and running through the operations called for in the program, to ascertain whether they accomplish the desired processing. This procedure catches programming errors without using machine time to discover their existence. Equally important is complete program documentation, including the operation manual (or run manual, as it is called) for the computer operator. In general, the programmer does not get to operate the computer while his program is tested. Instead, his program and test data are turned over to a computer operator at the test site. Obviously, the operating instructions are essential to a successful test.

The third element for program testing is a set of test data or input documents in machine-readable form (usually punched cards). The volume of test data need not be large. More important is the range of input item variation that it includes to test all capabilities of the program; i.e., each transaction type should be represented by one sample in the test deck (of cards).

A final note on individual program testing is in order. A new programmer may, with sublime confidence, assume that his program will run without difficulty when it is first tried. As he gains experience, that confidence will be tempered without being shaken. Until that experience is gained, he should be directed to include check points in his new program to simplify the task of locating program "bugs." These check points, or debugging aids, include memory dumps (snapshots of memory contents) at strategic points in the program or traces (motion pictures, as it were) of the processing steps in crucial areas of the program. As the programmer gains experience, he will come to include these aids without needing prompting, since if he leaves them out, he will be working in the dark in finding the troubles in his program.

After the programmers have verified the performance of their separate programs, these programs are taken in related groups for testing with data prepared by the systems analyst. These group tests determine whether or not system requirements are met; hence the use of system-oriented rather than program-oriented test data. Errors uncovered during group testing demand careful analysis to locate their causes and correct them. This analysis is needlessly complicated by the presence of an incompletely debugged program in the group, since the errors in that program look at first like group errors. As each group is proved out, the groups are combined or enlarged until all interacting programs for the new system are tested together. Upon successful completion of this total program group test, the system is ready for a shakedown run.

SYSTEM SHAKEDOWN RUN

The system shakedown run is both a final test of the system and a period of training in system operation. It exercises the whole new system if possible, including the personnel and procedures that precede and follow computer processing. Instead of using test data prepared by the programmers or the systems analyst, the shakedown run operates on real or "live" input data, which may be in either of two categories that depend upon the approach selected for the shakedown run. These two possible approaches are usually described as parallel operation versus pilot operation.

In parallel operation, the new system literally parallels the current system, taking in the same input data and producing equivalent outputs. The new system output is not put to actual use, however, but is compared against the results of current processing to validate the new system operation. Differences in output require investigation of both the new and current systems to pinpoint their causes.

Pilot operation also uses actual input data, but takes the preceding month's inputs rather than current ones. The results of the pilot operation are compared with the results of the current system for the same input data, again for the purpose of validating the new system with "live" data.

Pilot operation offers some advantages over parallel operation, particularly when run on the computer made available by the manufacturer for testing and conversion. First, pilot operation is less likely to disturb current operations because it is buffered by a one-month time lapse. Second, the pilot operation can be run on an accelerated time schedule, doing a month's work in considerably less than a calendar month. This accelerated schedule reduces the realism of operating practice, but allows earlier evaluation of new system operation and more time for correction of any deficiencies.

The system shakedown run, either pilot or parallel, is intended to reveal system errors while they can be corrected easily, before the new system is under pressure to maintain processing production. Other errors may crop up after the new system goes operational, but they should be few in number and small in importance if the shakedown run is thorough. Most of these errors stem from unanticipated input data items. These rare items are found only by running the system with "live" input data, preferably during the shakedown run. If any major corrections are made to the new system as a result of the shakedown run, another shakedown run should be made to demonstrate fault-free system operation.

MANUAL PROCEDURES

Concurrent with program preparation, the manual procedures to be followed outside the computer proper must also be developed. Generally, this task is handled by the systems analyst or his assistants. These manual procedures should be developed in the form of detailed procedures manuals, which can be used and followed carefully by untrained personnel. As the new system approaches completion, training in these procedures should be given to the personnel who will carry them out, using the manuals as "textbooks." This training program both familiarizes personnel with their tasks and serves to prove out the manuals. A second training cycle as part of the system shakedown is advisable, even if the manual steps are separated by several days from their ensuing computer operations.

The manual procedures must be particularly detailed for handling of items turned back by the computer, either because the items are different or because they contain errors or omissions.

These procedures for exceptional items are performed rather seldom, thus offering little practice in their execution. To prevent them from becoming a bottleneck in the new system, their handling procedures, like the instructions for a fire drill, must be thoroughly documented.

Associated with the development of manual procedures is the design of new forms for the system. Some of these forms are required to simplify data conversion (e.g., arrangement of input information for easier key punching). Other changes arise from consolidation of previously separate forms. Still others are needed to make best use of computer capabilities. For example, a computer line printer can produce a line that is 132 characters and spaces in width. Output forms may be redesigned to fit two output documents, side-by-side within this width, for faster computer preparation. Whatever the reason for their redesign, the new forms should be reviewed carefully by all their users before the designs are frozen. Another review by the representatives of forms suppliers can be helpful in suggesting further improvements or minor changes that can reduce the cost of these forms. Even then, only pilot orders should be placed for the new forms, since operation during the first production cycle with the new system may show the need for further changes.

MASTER FILE CONVERSION AND MAINTENANCE

The most underrated task in preparation for a new computer system is that of converting the master files and maintaining these files until the new system takes over that duty. If the current system is manually operated, the master files must be transcribed onto a machine-readable medium for submission to the new system. Punched cards are commonly selected, although perforated tape is equally suitable and may be cheaper to prepare. Facilities also exist for "key punching" directly onto magnetic tape, the medium on which the master files are likely to be maintained. Even if the current system uses a computer and has its master files on magnetic tape, the change to a new computer may still require transcription into new formats.

In addition to the mechanical problem of file transcription, the file conversion process usually involves consolidation of currently separate files and the creation of new files. When current files are consolidated, they must be purged of errors and duplicate records. A processing run on the computer or on punched cards can find and reject duplicate records. However, errors in the records can be found only by clerical checking (i.e., proofreading), performed either manually, by the file conversion programs, or by a combination of both methods. Since the file conversion programs will not anticipate all possible record errors, manual checking is essential. The staff for this manual checking will be more effective if it is familiar with the records and the significance of their entries, an argument in favor of using current employees for this task. One caution to be observed in this case is to assure these employees that they will not be fired when the conversion task is completed. One company failed to observe this caution and saw a three-month conversion task stretch out over three years, with the end still not in sight.

Care expended during file conversion yields dividends in smooth operation of the new system. The file editing for conversion will usually turn up some exceptional cases, which were unknown because of their rarity. These cases, which deviate from the file record standards set up by the systems analyst, must be dealt with in the programming effort just as other exceptional items. Catching these unusual file records now prevents their later appearance as mysterious problems in new system operation. Similarly, every record error purged during the conversion process is one less to be discovered by its disruptive effect on the new system.

Scheduling of the conversion task poses some tricky problems in connection with updating or file maintenance. If the conversion process for a single file is stretched out to reduce manpower requirements, a larger backlog of updating information is accumulated for application to the converted file. In the same way, early conversion of a file imposes the need for maintenance of that file over a longer time period. File conversion cannot start until the file editing, conversion, and updating programs have been written and tested. Beyond that limit, some compromise is needed between manpower loading and maintenance costs. It is imperative to maintain the converted files, applying changes to them on a regular schedule by using the computer made available by the manufacturer. Without updating, the converted files rapidly lose their value, wasting all the efforts expended on conversion. One approach to the updating problem assigns a separate staff to the editing and batching of data for file updating. When conversion starts on a file, applicable changes are shunted to the updating staff without entry into the file being converted. After the conversion staff has finished with a file, the updating staff becomes responsible for its maintenance until the new system goes into operation.

SITE PREPARATION AND SUPPLIES PROCUREMENT

Before the new system equipment is delivered, the site on which it is to be installed must be prepared for it. The computer manufacturer usually specifies the site facilities required or recommended for his equipment, and can assist materially in planning the equipment layout for maximum work efficiency. The physical facilities usually required for a computer installation include:

1. Electric power feeders and outlets
2. Air conditioning or humidity control equipment
3. File storage space and facilities, preferably fire-resistant
4. Auxiliary equipment such as file trucks, desks, tables, and schedule boards
5. Raised flooring for more efficient air conditioning and simplified interconnecting cable installation

The electric power requirements of the computer and of auxiliary units such as key punch machines are indicated in the manufacturer's literature. Once the equipment layout and configurations are determined, these requirements can be turned over to an electrical contractor for execution in conformity with local building codes and fire insurance regulations.

Air conditioning is not essential for current solid-state computers, since they dissipate comparatively little heat. However, equipment life and equipment reliability is improved by air conditioning, to say nothing of the performance of personnel who operate the computer. Further, the air-cleaning action of air conditioning reduces some of the operating difficulties of computers. Dust on magnetic tape or magnetic discs can cause serious reading errors, requring rereads to recover these errors. In addition, magnetic tape stores best within a restricted range of temperature and humidity, demanding air conditioning and humidity control equipment to protect the information stored on this medium. Similar considerations apply to punched cards and other machine-readable media, making air conditioning with humidity control generally advisable.

The facilities not supplied by the computer manufacturer should be discussed with his representative to solicit advice and suggestions. They should also be taken up with several suppliers. Some companies specialize in designing and equipping computer installations, providing the tables, trucks, and file storage equipment that contribute to an efficient installation. The suggestions they offer can forestall costly oversights in planning these support facilities. If facilities (such as raised flooring) are optional, it may pay to confer with computer users about the reasons for their choices in these areas. Ultimately, a system approach to these questions is worth while, evaluating each optional facility against its contribution to over-all system performance.

Coincident with site preparation, the operating supplies for the new system must be ordered far enough ahead of time for delivery with the new equipment. These supplies include punched cards, magnetic tapes, extra disc packs or magnetic card arrays (if these are used), and special printer forms. Stock items like standard punched cards (i.e., not specially printed) and printer forms should be ordered in quantities that reflect their projected use rate. Special forms, however, should be ordered in limited quantity, sufficient to cover the first production cycle by the new system and the delivery lag time on a reorder or changed order at the end of that cycle. As noted previously, these special forms may undergo changes in the light of experience during the first production cycle.

A system that uses magnetic tapes will need more tape reels than seems necessary at first sight, depending principally on file retention policies. For example, a one-reel master file requires at least three tape reels, one for the current master file, another for the previous master file (to allow reconstruction if the current file is destroyed), and a third, which will become the new current master file after the next update run. Note that two reels are not sufficient because the current master file is most endangered when it is used as input during an update run. If this file is processed weekly, the three-reel minimum provides file retention for just under two weeks; retention over a longer period (or number of update cycles) requires more tape reels.

In addition to master file storage, magnetic tapes are needed for program storage (often in duplicate for safety) and for working use (e.g., for sorting of transaction records). Again, file retention policies may call for the holding of transaction records on magnetic tape, although they are usually kept in submittal form (e.g., punched cards) and as written records. When disc packs or removable magnetic-card arrays are used for master file storage, magnetic tapes often serve for file retention, since the random access storage devices are too expensive for this function. If file retention and reconstruction capabilities are required, the master files are periodically written out on magnetic tape from the random storage device. Input transaction records may also be recorded on magnetic tape as they arrive, particularly if they are entered from keyboards without source documents or hard copies. With fallback file recordings and recordings of transactions, the master file can be reconstructed fairly easily if that should prove to be necessary. These recordings also offer useful historical information.

11

CHANGE-OVER TO THE NEW SYSTEM

With the preparations described in the preceding chapter, the new processing system should be ready to "go on the air" as soon as the new equipment is delivered and turned over to the user. Although the new system thus goes into operation immediately, it cannot be considered to be fully operational until it completes a full processing cycle, usually one month in duration. Operation during this first cycle is monitored closely, then reviewed for changes and improvements needed by the new system before it can be declared operational. The analyst and programmers assist at this review and the preceding monitoring. In fact, the programmers may leave their debugging aids in their programs until this review is completed, thereby simplifying the task of inserting and testing program changes. Only after this phase is completed can the new system be left to run without close surveillance, releasing the analyst and programmers for other tasks.

Cutover to the new system is often scheduled for the start of a fiscal year, provided equipment delivery and completion of the preparatory phase can be synchronized with that date. This cutover date leaves the old system with only the closing of the previous year's data to complete, and allows the new system, with its possibly changed accounting procedures, to start with a fresh slate. Complete cutover to the new system is particularly desirable if the old system is being run by temporary employees while regular personnel are retrained on the new system; this added labor cost can be terminated shortly after the new system starts up. Some companies have maintained their old system in parallel with the new system through the first month of processing. While this approach is perhaps overcautious and certainly expensive, it makes explicit the fact that the first processing cycle on the new system is that system's final test.

THE FIRST PROCESSING CYCLE

Continuous operation of the new system through its first processing cycle justifies the care expended in preparing for the new system. Anyone who has lived through the breakdown of a new system vows to prevent a recurrence of the experience. Programmers and systems analysts live the life of the damned in debugging the system under the baleful glare of management, losing sleep and growing beards as they work around the clock to restore normal operation. Labor costs skyrocket and labor efficiency plummets under these conditions, with hasty corrections often compounding the errors they were to correct. In short, any extreme in preparation for the new system is amply justified if it prevents these infernal events.

Usually, the new system does not escape unscathed by problems during its first processing cycle. Some problems arise from the changed procedures instituted for the new system. Other problems stem from inadequacies or oversights in these procedures and in the training of personnel to follow them. For example, company departments that submit data for processing may forget to observe the new submission due dates, thereby throwing the system off schedule. Similarly, a backlog may develop in some manual processing channel if its execution time or volume of data has been underestimated. Problems of this kind are almost inevitable, but are easily solved. More serious problems will, hopefully, not appear, since they should have been revealed during the system shakedown run.

Since the new system usually employs new equipment, the possibility of equipment malfunction always exists. The manufacturer cannot test his equipment in exactly the way it will be used, although his tests are as exhaustive as he can make them. Thus, when a program will not run on the new equipment, but ran perfectly during the system shakedown on an identical machine, the new equipment should be suspect immediately. Yet this suspicion is not entirely valid if the program was not thoroughly exercised during the system shakedown. Similarly, if the system produces unreasonable results, the input data should be the first suspect, but the computer and the program should also be checked. If the program debugging aids are left in during the first processing cycle, checks of the programs are greatly simplified. In particular, where the programs provide "check points" (i.e., recording of intermediate results for later analysis), these should be used to monitor system operation at the level of detail they provide.

Throughout the first processing cycle, the systems analyst and programmers should keep close watch on the system for the appearance of subtle faults or grounds for improvement to the system. At the same time, the data processing manager should observe and evaluate his operating personnel for possible additional training or even replacement if they prove inadequate to perform their tasks. In addition, he must evaluate the system processing schedule, revising it if actual run timings differ appreciably from their estimates. Of course run timing during this first processing cycle is likely to be pessimistic, since everyone involved with the system is still learning the operations required for efficient processing. Further, the program check-point operations add to run time. On the other hand, pessimistic run-time figures lead to more realistic schedules, with some slack for unanticipated difficulties. Finally, management should examine critically the support offered by the new system, with an eye to suggestions for improvement from its point of view.

Completion of the first processing cycle without a system breakdown does not certify the new system as fully successful. To arrive at this certification, new system performance must be monitored closely throughout that cycle, and then evaluated during a comprehensive review after the close of the cycle. This review determines what changes, if any, should be made to the system before the systems analyst or programmers, or both, are released for other applications. These changes may be prompted by management views of system performance, or by the analyst or programmers, to correct subtle faults in the system. This review after only one month of system operation will not uncover all improvements that should be made. In fact, computer centers that specialize in preparing large programming systems remain responsible for fault correction over the first year of operation, on the grounds that it takes at least that long for most faults to reveal themselves. (This latent error factor weighs heavily against "pioneering" on a newly introduced computer and its unproven software or programming system.) Business data processing systems, being less general in application, seldom conceal programming or operational faults for that long a time. Instead, these systems are subject to constant changes required by shifting business goals or needs, thus making the review that follows the first processing cycle only the first in a series of such reviews.

Unless the first processing cycle reveals some grievous faults in the new system, the attitude during the review should be evolutionary rather than revolutionary. A serious fault will require system redesign and may even cause reinstatement of the old system during the redesign phase; thorough preparation and system test should make this most unlikely. When the new system successfully performs its mandatory tasks, changes proposed after the first cycle should be confined to tinkering, if only to preserve that capability. This caution at the end of the first processing cycle must be weighed against the availability of the systems analyst and the programmers to make changes at this time. Thus, suggested changes can be made more readily before these people are released; yet the changes should not jeopardize the mandatory processing capabilities of the new system.

It should be obvious that a similar period of close monitoring and final review is needed to evaluate any changes made following the first processing cycle. In particular, the data processing manager should refine his run times after each processing cycle, as a means of rating his operating personnel. Once the system is declared operational (after the first or second processing cycle), the number of system changes per cycle will decline, making the post-cycle review less formal and, possibly, less important. However, any significant change to the system must be subjected to the same kind of post-cycle review to determine its effectiveness.

EXTENSION TO OTHER APPLICATIONS

When the new processing system is declared to be operational, maintenance of its programs is usually turned over to a new group (however small) of programmers, who make the minor changes called for by subsequent business requirements. The original task force team made up by the systems analyst and the first-time programmers are freed by this declaration to tackle other applications for addition to the new system. Of course the programmers on loan from the computer manufacturer are usually recalled at this point, but the newly trained or hired programmers on the user's staff remain available to handle these additional applications.

Ideally, any new application for a computer system is taken through the full process of a feasibility study, i.e., system design effort before any programming begins. If the new processing system is already installed and operating, this effort is considerably simplified, both because the new system equipment has been chosen and because the added application need not justify much if any added equipment. Yet a thorough study of the new application as called for in the feasibility study (Chapter 5) and in system design (Chapter 7) is fully justified to simplify the resulting programming effort. Again, ideally, some of or all this investigation will have been done as part of the effort for the basic new system, if only to assure the integration of the added application. If not, the investigation should stress these integration requirements. As noted earlier, this integration of previously disparate operations has been of greater value to computer users than any economies that stemmed directly from the computer proper.

The investigation of new applications can be carried out by the systems analyst, assisted by the programmers assigned to him. Generally, the analyst performs the information gathering and codification, leaving to the programmers the system design task which precedes their programming efforts. Just as with the first applications for the new system, these added applications must go through the same preparatory steps before their processing is cut over onto the new system. Individual programs are tested separately, then in groups if that is applicable, and finally in a system shakedown run to establish confidence in the new processing system. Again, the new application should be reviewed after the close of the first processing cycle, before the analyst and programmers are turned loose on yet another new application. As can be seen, this process repeats until all justifiable processing is transferred to the new system, leaving only refinements to be added. Often, at that point, the larger cycle of development of a new "new system" must begin, to accommodate either the accumulation of company growth and change or the advances in computer design and pricing, or both. The data processing function deserves as much continued evaluation and review as any other cost or product center within an operating company. Since the data processing function embodies much of the company's policy decisions and provides one of the most useful tools for management, it certainly deserves the continued surveillance by management, to be discussed in the next chapter.

12

MANAGEMENT'S LIFE
WITH THE COMPUTER

The adoption of computer processing simplifies management's tasks in directing current business activities, provided management plays its full role in the development of the processing system. In the application areas turned over to the computer, management policies are carried through automatically because they are embodied in the processing system. In addition, the management information system incorporated in the processing structure provides timely information in useful form. However, management has a continuing role to play in connection with its computer system, both in the preparation of new applications to be added to the system and in the monitoring of system operation. The data processing manager, running a service organization within the company, tends to resist changes because they can disturb his carefully planned schedules. Yet changes are sure to be needed if only to match the changes in management goals and business situations. Accordingly, management must continually review the effectiveness of its computer system as a management tool, keeping the system responsive to its changing needs.

Management may become involved with the computer for planning future business activities as well as in directing current activities. With proper programming, the computer can be used to *simulate* or model a real-world situation or a complex process. These simulation techniques are widely used by the military and by large companies for comparative evalution of plans to meet the modeled

178 SYSTEM INSTALLATION AND OPERATION

situation, or for optimization of modeled processes. They can be equally useful to smaller companies if the cost of model development can be justified or if an adaptable model is available (e.g., from the computer manufacturer or a program library). Simulation techniques yield valuable and often unforeseen results, within the limits of the model's validity.

With continued use of the computer, management gains considerable sophistication about the computer's capabilities and limitations for its company. This learning process leads inevitably to a complete redesign of the processing system, hopefully in conjunction with the planning for the next system. As noted earlier, the computer in the current system will be made obsolete by the growth of the applications it handles, not by the introduction of newer and faster computers. However, if obsolescence from growth is approaching, management may do better to shorten the life of the current system, changing to a newer and cheaper computer before the current computer is swamped. Management will participate in the planning for the next system with greater understanding of the computer's impact on its organization, leading to the development of a significantly better system because it will be better matched to the company's requirements.

Having introduced three rather large topics, the rest of this chapter is devoted to further discussion of them. As will be seen, management's life with the computer remains at least as lively as that life was before the computer entered the business scene.

MANAGEMENT'S CONTINUING ROLE

The role of management in the planning of applications to be added to the computer is obvious enough to require no further comment. Less obvious is the need for continued management attention to applications already on the computer. The temptation is to let these applications run undisturbed, a temptation that is encouraged by the data processing manager. He is prompt to point out the costs and inconveniences caused by changes. They demand programming time, program test time on the computer, and possible training of personnel in new procedures. Even worse from his point of view, they may cause changes in the operating schedule of his smoothly running system. Unfortunately, the data processing manager's goals are not always identical with his company's goals. Smooth operation of the computer system, while desirable, is not the ultimate criterion for the system. What is significant is the effectiveness of the computer system as a management tool, a criterion that is of less importance to the data processing manager.

Company management must use the data processing manager to administer the computer system and to determine the feasibility of changes, including the costs of making those changes. However, the declaration that a change cannot be made is arbitrary unless it can be backed up by comprehensible explanations. In fact, the data processing manager should never deliver this kind of judgment if he wishes to retain the confidence of his superiors. Instead, when management submits a request for a change to the current system, he must strive to find the best and cheapest way to fill that request, then report his estimate to management for a decision that weighs the value of the change against its cost. The data processing manager is in no position to establish this value. Despite his topline position in his own group, he and his department serve as staff to the rest of the company.

Management should understand the computer system well enough to avoid making "impossible" demands on it. This is not to say that the company president must be conversant with the latest computer lingo. Instead, he and his close associates should know broadly what the computer can and cannot do. Management is concerned with over-all company operations and profitability; the data processing manager has more specific concerns and more limited understanding of over-all company goals. Yet he and management must know something of each other's problems if they are to communicate effectively. It is hoped that this book contributes to the president's understanding of his company's data processing operations. It is also to be hoped that management will be thus armed to insist on its goals rather than being silenced by ignorance and fear of the computer.

One common area of "disagreement" between management and

the data processing manager is that of exception handling. The data processing manager is likely to consider exceptional transactions as comparatively unimportant, without any grounds for that judgment other than the rarity of these transactions. Management may well take a different view, considering the rare million-dollar order in a run of ten-dollar orders, or the odd item in an order from a large-volume customer, to be extremely important. To the data processing manager, these rare items do not justify the cost of expeditious handling because that cost is high in comparison with the cost of handling high-volume items. It should be apparent that he may have a narrow viewpoint in this respect.

As business requirements change, so must the computer system change to match them. These requirements are determined by management and passed on for implementation by the computer system. The inertia of the operating department tends to resist these changes, perhaps by overestimating the cost of their implementation. Management must guard against this inertia by bringing to bear some broad understanding of the computer system. With this understanding, management can insist on responsiveness of the computer system to its changing needs without imposing unnecessary burdens on that system. Indeed, unless this understanding is present, management may make so many unessential changes as to disable the system or to raise its cost above the justifiable level.

SIMULATION

All the various simulation techniques that can be used with a computer depend on the development of a model of the process or situation to be simulated. This model is usually formulated as a set of mathematical equations, since these are most easily adapted to the computer. Perhaps the classic example of computer simulation deals with the warehousing problem; i.e., the problem of optimum inventory levels at each of several widely separate warehouses, for maximum profit, minimum investment, or minimum delivery lag after order receipt. This problem and others like it are dealt with by *linear programming*, a technique that manipulates a model of the situation to determine the best values of controllable variables (e.g., warehouse stock levels) to achieve a best result (e.g., one of the goals cited above). The mathematical model relates the factors that interact to yield the results and to weight their contributions to those results.

The field of model development is usually described under the title of *operations research*. An operation or process to be modeled is studied closely, with measurements of input and output variables, to determine the relevance and importance of each. When the study has progressed sufficiently, a trial model is constructed; i.e., the relations among input and output variables are reduced to a set of equations. The trial model is then tested against what is being modeled to measure its validity. In effect, the model is used to predict what the real situation does in response to the same inputs, checking the prediction against the real response. The degree of agreement is the only measure of model validity. If that agreement is insufficient to be useful, the model is modified, possibly by the inclusion of more input variables in more equations, until it proves sufficiently predictive (or accurate) for useful application. At this point, the model can be transformed into a computer program for rapid exercise of model operation by the computer. If the model is simple enough mathematically (i.e., linear), linear programming is used to optimize the controlled variables with respect to any one uncontrolled variable such as return on investment. Otherwise, the model is exercised on the computer with many different values of each controlled variable, to demonstrate their effects on the model output. The computer will not yield clearly optimum solutions in this case, but they can be found by examining the results of the many simulation runs.

Operations research is restricted to situations in which all variables are measurable in one way or another. As a result, it has only limited application to situations that involve imponderables (e.g., marketing strategy in a competitive field). This limitation is relieved somewhat by *gaming theory*, a simulation technique used widely by the military in war gaming and by some large companies for the application just cited. In gaming theory, the mathematical model is usually fairly simple (mostly because the theory cannot yet cope with complex situations), and the resulting weighting factors, called *scoring factors*, are assigned on an intuitive basis. For example, complete domination of a sales field is scored as 100 per cent, complete loss of the field scores 0 per cent, and intermediate results are scored in accordance with the score assigner's judgment. Luckily, it has been impossible so far to determine the validity of the gaming theory models used in war gaming; the same question is still open in the use of gaming theory for business applications. The proponents of gaming theory in both fields assert its training value, offering practice in decision making under pressure.

As a general rule, computer predictive power through simulation is no better than the validity of the model on which its predictions are based. Yet, even a less than absolutely valid model can yield predictions of value to management. Like a young but inexperienced ballplayer, the computer speed can cover some model errors by trying out a great variety of situations in a very short time, to reveal trends if not exact predictions. Often these trends are quite surprising, forcing management to reconsider its ground rules for decision making. Further, if the model is suspected of inaccuracy, its structure can be perturbed with respect to each source of inaccuracy, thus showing their relative effects on model results. In this way, levels of confidence are developed in different aspects of the model and in different ranges of result values. Simulation works best with fully valid models, but less perfect models should not be barred from use.

THE NEXT TIME AROUND

The successful user of computer processing is, in some ways, like a narcotics addict; he is "hooked" on the advantages of the computer and unwilling, if not unable, to forego them. As a result, his first computer system will not be his last system. Instead, as his company grows and spreads, his computer processing system will undergo corresponding changes and even complete replacement to accommodate the expansion of his applications. Interestingly, successful computer users put as much planning, or more, into their second system as they did their first, profiting from the experience they gained with the first system to develop an even better replacement. Management is more sophisticated about computer usage after its first try and more aware of the benefits to be obtained from computer processing.

The emphasis throughout this book has been on the justification of a computer system on an economic basis and on the rationalization of company operations to take full advantage of computer capabilities. That emphasis is equally applicable when considering a second system, or any succeeding system. The surest way to lose money through the use of computers is to change to each new model as it is introduced. The next best way is to stick with an outgrown system for long after the time needed to recover its costs. If management considers its computer replacement decision just as it considers the replacement of production machinery, the economics of the decision are put on the right footing.

We turn now to the rationalization of company activities for best use of the computer (described earlier as the application of computer "logic" to company operations) because there is some confusion over this question within the computer fraternity. The point throughout this book has been that the computer allows and even demands centralized processing of the information flow for most or all company activities. This point is often extended to show that the computer allows centralized control of decentralized operations within the company. The confusion arises from a further extension which has the computer demand such centralized control, an extension that is not valid. The confusion is based on identification of information flow with the processes or activities that produce that flow.

It is true that very large companies resorted to decentralization when their size made central control inefficient and that this trend was reversed, even as company sizes increased, by the introduction of computers; i.e., the computer allows centralized control in situations whose size or complexity make such control impossible without computers. As an example, U.S. Steel recentralized its structure after it adopted computers extensively. At about the same time as it tied its divisions together with data communications links, it recentralized its organizational structure, leaving some seven division presidents to seek new positions, surely one of the highest levels of impact by "automation." The counterexample is provided by Westinghouse, which established a centralized management information system for its corporate staff to direct its diversified and decentralized manufacturing divisions. The computer processing of information by Westinghouse is at least as centralized as that by U.S. Steel, yet Westinghouse maintains its company activities on a decentralized basis.

The same range of choice is available to any company, whatever its size. The computer can implement tightly centralized control of company operations; equally, it can implement a comprehensive management information system while servicing the processing requirements of decentralized company activities without imposing centralized control of these activities beyond the limits established by management. In short, a computer almost demands centralized information processing, which in turn makes possible a centralized company control without requiring it. The choice between centralized and decentralized control is thus left where it belongs, in the hands of management. The computer serves management's needs and goals in either case.

The question of centralized versus decentralized control is pertinent when considering the next computer system for a smaller company because the choice may affect the cost of its comprehensive management information system. As smaller and cheaper computers are introduced, more companies will face the alternatives of a large central computer with remote data communications terminals versus small satellite computers at remote locations, tied together with a smaller central computer. The first alternative is ideal with centralized control, removing all computing capabilities from the remote locations. On the other hand, the satellite adjuncts of the central computer can satisfy either requirement and offer better reaction to system degradation (i.e., the failure of one or more system elements, either the central computer or a satellite). The use of satellite computers at remote locations need not weaken central control or central information monitoring if all programming by the central computer staff adheres to standards that require the transmission of all pertinent information to the central site.

Another development, which will loom larger in the near future, is the proliferation of computer centers that offer time-shared use of their facilities. The computer fraternity is already talking about six to ten "information processing utilities" nationwide to serve all but 10 per cent of processing needs within the country. (That excluded 10 per cent covers the very large computer users who would, presumably, establish their own internal "utilities.") Whether or not this prediction is fulfilled, small computer users should examine the relative merits of their on-premises systems versus large time-shared systems. (As mentioned in Chapter 3, ten such facilities are offered as this is being written; initial cost figures are also cited there.) Part-time use of a large computer may be more profitable than full-time use of a smaller one. For example, a full hour of operation from a remote terminal in an experimental time-sharing system incurred a total cost of 51 cents for computer time (which was billed at $300 per hour), exclusive of terminal- and communications-line costs. The same operation on a smaller and cheaper on-premises computer (e.g., billed at $14 per hour) could easily run up a larger computer time cost because the smaller computer shows a higher cost per elementary operation. Computers certainly justify the old saw that "it's cheaper by the dozen." Further, a large computer can perform operations that are not feasible on a smaller computer. When part-time use of a large computer offers capabilities that are unavailable on smaller machines and offers them at lower cost than can be achieved with smaller machines, part-time use of a large computer is worth serious investigation.

To conclude this consideration of the next pass through computer system investigation, development, and selection, it is worth while to repeat the fundamental import of computer processing for management.

The computer can stem the rising cost of clerical functions in any business operation, displacing personnel in the short run but meeting the long-term shortage of trained or trainable personnel for clerical functions brought on by increasing demand. The computer can also, with intelligent application, integrate and consolidate information processing within a business, yielding significant savings by eliminating duplicated steps in decentralized information processing and by minimizing transcription errors. Management must always treat the computer as another (albeit rather powerful) tool that serves its needs, speeding the flow of information through the company, accelerating company response to customer demands on a short-time cycle, and matching company posture to the business environment on a long-time cycle. Above all, management must use the computer rather than being used by it.

APPENDIX I

The Rent-or-Buy Decision

by Jerome Gartner, LL.B.

Computer purchase has become a mystique comparable to judging the value of modern art works. Otherwise objective businessmen are awed by the technology of the computer field and have chosen in the main to rent rather than purchase computers. The author believes that contrary to current practice most computer users and especially second-time users would benefit financially by purchasing. First-time computer users must decide whether they have selected with sufficient care the right type of equipment for their needs. Renting is expensive insurance against a grievous error in selecting suitable equipment.

TECHNOLOGICAL vs. FUNCTIONAL OBSOLESCENCE

The bugaboo of obsolescence needs resolution before objective consideration can be given to purchasing computer equipment.

There are two kinds of obsolescence—functional and technological. Functional obsolescence is the familiar problem of the machine becoming more costly to maintain and operate than to replace with new equipment. The intricate design of computer equipment led many users to believe that the expected physical life of the machinery would be relatively short, and computer history of less than ten years in production gave no basis for establishing a work life. Today we know the main frame and much of the peripheral equipment are extremely sturdy. So sturdy that a major insurance company in the Midwest is still using a first generation vacuum tube computer (*circa* 1954) although they must inventory their own spare parts. With the present use of solid state parts in computer equipment, the machines in many cases exceed substantially the present estimate of life for depreciation purposes. Further indication of this durability is the large reductions in maintenance contract costs for purchased computers.

Technological obsolescence, on the other hand, can occur at any time as marvelous new improvements are put into production. The new System/360 and its competitors are cheaper and faster with substantially larger capacities than the predecessor models. Yet users of satisfactory systems did not switch immediately to the newly announced equipment; the advantages did not outweigh the cost of change-over.

Another technological improvement is time-sharing, where a number of computer users share rental time on a huge computer. One of the axioms of computers is that the larger the machine, the less the cost of running a given program. Time-sharing, by users of large computers, will be an important segment of the computer market. However, time-sharing is only now being pioneered; it is not likely to be sufficiently developed for economical use for the next several years.

In fact, it appears unlikely that any radically new innovations will be introduced before 1972 or later. The reasons are several. Main frame equipment—the costliest part of a computer—is radically faster than most peripheral equipment; i.e., 2 million computations per second against print-out at ten lines per second. Much time and research money are necessary to improve speed of peripheral equipment. Until this is done it is unlikely that faster main frames will be introduced. Further, the new generation of computers is being produced by mass production methods requiring extremely costly machinery. Only sizable production will justify the development cost.

INDIRECT FINANCIAL CONSIDERATIONS

There are indirect financial advantages to purchasing your computer.

By owning the computer, the company may easily utilize unneeded second-shift time to enter into reciprocal arrangements with companies possessing similar configurations to secure backup time in case of breakdown or peak period jam-ups.

There is great value in having inexpensive unused computer time available in-house. Most rental contracts provide added costs for use in excess of one-shift time, and thereby put a high premium on exceeding the contractual amount of hours. A company initially programs only its basic needs on a computer.

Management is freer to experiment with new uses on a computer, where the additional per-hour cost is relatively small for computer time. Where the computer is owned, and running costs and amortization are already allocated to the basic company needs, out-of-pocket costs for extra computer time become very cheap, perhaps $5.00 per hour including the console operator.

FINANCIAL FACTORS

Assuming the nonfinancial questions are answered satisfactorily, the decision to buy, rent, or lease the computer and peripheral equipment depends on the most economical method for the company.

Below are eight factors which collectively should control the decision to rent or buy. Leasing, which is briefly mentioned, is basically a form of renting.

To clarify the explanation, a hypothetical example has been used; namely, the company is considering acquisition of a computer main frame for $100,000 purchase price. Maintenance, parts, and labor, $250 a month constant up to seventy-two months. Rental of the main frame would be $2,500 per month, including maintenance. The main frame would be depreciated on a five-year life.

1. Depreciation reserves and permanently retained depreciation
2. Right to choose estimated depreciable life
3. Calculation of annual depreciation and accelerated formulas
4. Optimum depreciable life
5. Salvage and end-life value
6. Rental or lease vs. purchase
7. Use of borrowed money to purchase computers
8. Seven per cent investment credit

Recent government tax policy has been to promote economic growth in the United States by encouraging business to expand their capital outlays for new equipment; in the past, the tax laws have been amended for this through changes in a series of interacting tax provisions and regulations. The effect of these changes is to provide strong monetary incentives for purchase of new tangible equipment, including computer equipment.

The dollar-cost of purchasing machinery when the government is a half partner (48 per cent federal tax plus state and local tax may make the percentage significantly higher than 50 per cent) depends on determining as accurately as possible the company's cost in after-tax dollars. To the extent the company can effectively utilize government tax concessions favoring one form of acquisition over another, the cost of purchase of new equipment can be substantially lowered in after-tax dollar cost. The savings may be so substantial to the company as to overcome its reluctance to purchase, based on other considerations. The mathematical and tax computations are too complicated for this appendix to do more than present the outlines of the problem which each company must weigh individually, after consultation with their tax, legal, and financial consultants.

1. *Depreciation Reserve*

The dominant factor in tax saving is depreciation reserve. This has come to have two meanings—each important to the company's financial health. First, depreciation reserve represents a method of computing wasting assets which must be replaced when worn out, if the company is to continue in business.

Second, depreciation reserve created by reductions in the company's taxes becomes part of the assets of the business, either for other new equipment or other needs. As a practical matter, nobody puts the depreciation reserves in a sock—or even maintains liquid assets solely for replacement needs which may be ten years off.

The government, as a 50 per cent partner in tax deductible depreciation reserves, can increase substantially the cash available in the business; to the extent that there are taxable profits and, through the tax loss, carry-forward and carry-back provisions, there need only be profits over a period of several years rather than in any given year. Monies not taxed and thereby retained in the business represent increased capital. The significance is shown by financial analysts who now compute the value of a company's stock by calculating both after-tax profits and cash flow. Cash flow is after-tax profits plus untaxed funds retained in the business—untaxed because of depreciation reserve deductions from taxable income.

There are important savings in buying and being able to take depreciation. The most important is the company's ability to retain cash in the business, indefinitely—if the business continues to purchase new equipment. A level of depreciable purchases of $1 million per year over a period of years should result in permanently retaining $500,000 in the business which otherwise would have been paid out in taxes.

2. *Right to Choose Estimated Depreciation Life*

Present depreciation rules permit a variety of formulas to be used by the company to suit their own needs:
  (a) Approximately 75 broad depreciation groups and estimated lives were established to cover all depreciable tangible property, and a company may choose the fitting one without later question by the government. The usual group for computer lives is ten years, although other categories with different lives are used.
  (b) Under the *Procedure* adopted by the Treasury in 1962, a company is free to choose its own estimated depreciable life for a computer, of which depreciable life forms the basis for the annual deductions. A company may pick any reasonable period of time

for estimated life, and the government, under a three-year freeze policy adopted in 1962 and now extended for another year, agrees not to question the basis of estimated life within the period. Thereafter, the correctness of the estimated life is governed by adherence to reserve ratios which, in effect, ensure the reasonable relationship of the company's estimate of depreciation and the company's actual practice in retiring equipment and purchasing new equipment.

3. Calculation of Annual Depreciation and Accelerated Formulas

The company can choose the method for computing depreciation annually; these examples are based on an estimated five-year life.
(a) Sum of the years' digits (first year 5/15—33 per cent; first two years 9/15—60 per cent)
(b) 150 per cent of straight line (first year 30 per cent)
(c) Straight line (first year 20 per cent)
(d) Double declining balance (first year 40 per cent)
The advantage of the sum of the years' digits method over the more familiar straight-line depreciation method, and other accelerated methods, is that heavier depreciation deductions result in the first years, based on a five-year life.

4. Optimum Depreciable Life

The depreciation deduction is the major factor in deciding whether it is more economic to purchase instead of renting. The decision on what depreciation basis is used is also dependent on the method used to depreciate the company's other tangible personal property. Maximum depreciation benefit may not be realized if the present company accounting procedure is based on maximizing other tax advantages.

The tax laws often force the company to choose among a complexity of tax advantages offered by competing tax sections. By choosing a five-year life and calculations based on sum-of-the-digits method, the company gains the advantage of heavy depreciation deductions in the early years of ownership. However, some of the 7 per cent investment credit is lost. Only machinery depreciated over an eight-year life is eligible for all of the investment credit. A five-year life makes the purchase eligible for only one-third of the investment credit. There is also an additional first-year depreciation allowance, intended primarily to benefit small businesses, which may be applicable in some cases to computer purchase.

5. *Salvage and End-Life Value*

The above depreciation formulas are based on depreciating 100 per cent of the computer equipment in five years. This is permissible under the government's regulations which permit the company to ignore up to 10 per cent of the salvage value. So, if the estimate is that the main frame will be worth $10,000 at the end of five years, for tax purposes it may be treated as if it will have no value.

Estimated usable life cannot be too extravagantly short because if the equipment is sold, all gain over depreciated value is taxed as ordinary income instead of capital gains as formerly.

A company at the end of five years would have several choices to maximize the value of the computer:

(a) Make a charitable gift to a university where, with certain exceptions, total market value of the gift would be tax deductible;
(b) Maintain equipment as stand-by or backup for new computer;
(c) Apply equipment for use in other functions, whose present cost would not justify new equipment. The federal government has successfully applied this approach to all its computer installations and has organized a program of passing equipment on to lower priority agencies and uses as new equipment is procured.

6. *Rental or Lease* vs. *Purchase*

A straight rental with no purchase option agreement is eligible for 100 per cent tax deduction. Some rental plans provide a purchase option. If the rental payments include some percentage or fraction of cost applicable to the value of the purchase option, then the rental payments are not fully deductible as an expense.

Purchase price is not fully deductible from income in the year of purchase except to the extent depreciation and other tax sections like the investment credit are applicable in that year.

From the user's standpoint, leasing from outside companies is a form of rental. As an additional indication of the value of purchasing, some of the major leasing companies have sufficient faith to lease computers to users at 10 per cent or more below manufacturers' rental charges in the belief that the remaining value after the lease period will be sufficient to return them a nice profit.

7. *Use of Borrowed Money to Purchase Computers*

Purchase of a computer with borrowed money is the most economical form, if reasonable terms for borrowing can be obtained. The banks today consider computer main frame equipment good collateral for loans. 80 per cent of cost is considered reasonable which in the example means only $20,000 cash is required. Interest costs are tax deductible and the government pays approximately half.

8. *Seven Per Cent Investment Credit*

The government subsidizes purchases of equipment by the 7 per cent investment credit, which applies in full for approximately $350,000 of purchases a year, and covers bad earning years by carry-forward and carryback provisions; and it further provides for additional credits where purchases exceed $350,000 and company income is substantial. Since manufacturers can pass through the credit to the lessee where equipment is rented instead of purchased, the 7 per cent credit does not usually affect the decision to rent or buy. It does effectively represent a deduction in the price to the company.

CONCLUSION

The author's belief that computer equipment should be purchased is supported by the detailed studies and investigation of the U.S. government which arrived at the conclusion several years ago that all government computer equipment should be purchased, not rented.

The research was based on costs which did not include the added benefit of depreciation and tax savings which are available to private industry.

The example in Appendix II assumes that a company is considering acquisition of a computer main frame for $100,000 purchase price. A maintenance contract, including parts and labor, would cost $250 a month constant up to 72 months. Rental of the main frame would be $2,500 per month, including maintenance. The main frame would be depreciated on a five-year life and have a salvage value of $5,000.

APPENDIX II

Computer Main Frame: Purchase vs. Rental, 1966–1971

Table 1.

PURCHASE OF MAIN FRAME OF COMPUTER VS. RENTAL, 1966

Computer installed on November 15, 1965. Loan and rental payments start January 1, 1966.

Expenses		Purchase	Rental
January 1, 1966 down payment		$20,000	
Year 1966 service contract (parts and labor)		3,000	
Payments on $80,000 (Loan five years @ 6%)		18,400	
Total expenses 1966		$41,400	$30,000
Deductions from Income			
One-half year depreciation 1965 (permitted if consistent with present accounting procedure) using sum of digits at first-year rate of 5/15 of $100,000	$16,667		
First half-year depreciation, year 1966	16,667		
Second half-year depreciation 1966 (at second-year rate 4/15)	13,334		
Service contract	3,000		
Interest deductions	2,400		
Total tax deductions	52,068		
@ 50% tax rate	26,034		15,000
Plus 7% investment credit (with five-years life eligible for one-third—2.333%)	$ 2,333		$ 7,000
Total tax savings		28,367	22,000
After-tax dollar-cost, 1966 (first year)		$13,033	$ 8,000

NOTE: The calculations used in this example are approximations.

Table 2.
PURCHASE OF MAIN FRAME OF COMPUTER vs. RENTAL, 1967

Expenses		*Purchase*	*Rental*
Loan (amortization and interest)	$18,400		
Service contract	3,000		
Total expenses 1967		$21,400	$30,000
Deductions from Income			
First half-year depreciation	13,334		
Second half-year	10,000		
Service contract	3,000		
Interest deductions	2,400		
Total deductions	$28,734		
@ 50% tax rate		14,367	15,000
After-tax dollar-cost, 1967 (second year)		$ 7,033	$15,000

Table 3.
PURCHASE OF MAIN FRAME OF COMPUTER vs. RENTAL, 1968

Expenses		*Purchase*	*Rental*
Loan	$18,400		
Service contract	3,000		
Total expenses 1968		$21,400	$30,000
Deductions from Income			
First half-year 1968 depreciation	10,000		
Second half-year 1968 depreciation	6,667		
Service contract	3,000		
Interest	2,400		
Total deductions	$22,067		
@ 50% tax rate		11,034	15,000
After-tax dollar-cost, 1968 (third year)		$10,366	$15,000

Table 4.
PURCHASE OF MAIN FRAME OF COMPUTER VS. RENTAL, 1969

Expenses		*Purchase*	*Rental*
Loan	$18,400		
Service contract	3,000		
Total expenses 1969		$21,400	$30,000
Deductions from Income			
First half-year 1969 depreciation	6,667		
Second half-year 1969 depreciation	1,666		
Service contract	3,000		
Interest	2,400		
Total deductions	$13,733		
@ 50% tax rate		6,867	15,000
After-tax dollar-cost, 1969 (fourth year)		$14,533	$15,000

Table 5.
PURCHASE OF MAIN FRAME OF COMPUTER VS. RENTAL, 1970

Expenses		*Purchase*	*Rental*
Loan	$18,400		
Service contract	3,000		
Total expenses 1970		$21,400	$30,000
Deductions from Income			
First half-year depreciation	3,333		
Service contract	3,000		
Interest	2,400		
Total deductions	$5,400		
@ 50% tax rate		2,700	15,000
After-tax dollar-cost, 1970 (fifth year)		$18,700	$15,000

Table 6.

PURCHASE OF MAIN FRAME OF COMPUTER VS. RENTAL, 1971

Expenses		*Purchase*	*Rental*
Service contract	$3,000		
Total expenses 1971		$3,000	$30,000
Deductions from Income			
Service contract	3,000		
@ 50% tax rate		1,500	15,000
After-tax dollar-cost, 1971 (sixth year)		$1,500	$15,000

Table 7. SUMMARY

Five-Year After-Tax Dollar Expenditures

1966	first	13,033	8,000
1967	second	7,033	15,000
1968	third	10,366	15,000
1969	fourth	14,533	15,000
1970	fifth	18,700	15,000
Five-year total		63,665	68,000
	sixth	1,500	15,000
Six-year total		$65,165	$83,000
Savings on purchase after two years			$ 2,934
(fully paid-for computer) five years			4,335
(fully paid-for computer) six years			17,835

NOTE: Annual cash outlay requirements for purchase do not differ greatly from rental. The first-year purchase is higher by $5,000, but by the end of the second year it is $2,934 lower than rental cash outlay requirements.

GLOSSARY

The following list of terms used in the computer field is not intended to be exhaustive or definitive. It does, however, include most of the terms of technical significance used in this book, defining these terms here to spare the reader from turning to another source for their meanings. Italicized words within definitions refer to other entries in the glossary.

absolute address: The address of a storage location as recognized by the computer; e.g., pigeonhole 279 rather than the "second one from the corner."

access time: The time between specification of a storage location and access to it for reading or writing; usually shorter than the *storage-cycle* time for computer *main storage.*

address (n): The designation of a storage location, comparable to a house number that identifies a residence; *see also* absolute address, relative address, and symbolic address.

address (v): To refer to a storage location.

alphameric: See alphanumeric.

alphanumeric: The letters of the alphabet, the digits 0 through 9, and certain punctuation marks, for a total of from 48 to 64 discrete symbols, depending upon the system used; *alphameric* is another name for this set of symbols, usually represented in six-bit *BCD* code or eight-bit *EBCDIC* code.

ASCII: American Standards Code for Information Interchange, an approved standard code based on teletype code, but expanded to 7 *bits* per *character,* thus allowing up to 128 discrete characters; an extended version of this code, using 8 bits per character, accommodates 256 discrete characters, like *EBCDIC,* but the code patterns for each character differ from those in EBCDIC.

assembly: The process of translation by the computer of a *symbolic program* into an absolute program which it can execute.

background: The *batch processing* performed by a *time-sharing* system "behind" its *demand processing* load to fill the gaps between demands.

backup: A comparable *hardware* array available in case of failure of on-premises equipment; often arranged on a reciprocal basis among neighboring computer users.

batch processing: Conventional computer usage in which the information to be processed is accumulated outside the computer and then submitted as a batch for most efficient processing (from the computer point of view); contrast with *demand processing;* note that some data are naturally batched, such as periodic payroll data.

BCD: Binary-coded decimal, which see.

benchmark problem: A problem submitted to competing suppliers of processing facilities for a comparative evaluation of their performance of said problem; a standard measurement of the performance of the delivered computer system as compared to supplier's claims.

binary: Literally dual, or two-valued; the binary number system is based on the number 2, just as the decimal number system is based on the number 10; computers use binary numbers internally in one form or another because on-off devices (having the values 1 if "on" or 0 if "off") are used in their construction.

binary-coded decimal (BCD): One form of information representation within a computer, coding (i.e., representing) each decimal digit by 4 binary bits; BCD is extended to include letters of the alphabet and punctuation marks by using two extra *bits,* called *zone bits;* this 6-bit BCD code can represent 64 different symbols (digits, letters, punctuation marks), although some equipment recognizes only 48 of the 6-bit combinations as valid symbols.

bit: Abbreviation of *binary* digit; has either of two values, 1 or 0, as opposed to a decimal digit, which may have any value from 0 through 9; also, the smallest information unit, a "yes" or "no" decision.

block: A group of *records, words,* or *storage* locations, treated as a physical unit; a block on magnetic tape, for example, may contain several logical records, which are combined into the one block for greater efficiency in information transfer.

byte: Generally, any separately manipulatable group of bits within a *binary fixed word,* simplifying the packing and unpacking of these words; more specifically, in a large group of computers, a unit of information 8 bits in length which can represent a *character* (one out of 256) in *EBCDIC,* two decimal digits in *packed format* (4 bits per digit), or any value up to 255 ($2^8 - 1$) in binary form; larger binary values may be represented by groups of *bytes.*

character: A symbol representable in *BCD* or *EBCDIC* code; usually also a 6-*bit* group that represents one of the 64 possible symbols representable by that many bits or an 8-bit group that represents one of the 256 possible symbols representable by that many bits.

check point: Generally, a point at which a program can be safely interrupted and from which it can be resumed; more specifically, a point within a program preceding an untested portion of the program that may destroy previously developed results of processing.

COBOL: Common business oriented language.

coding: The second phase of programming which turns a machine-executable problem solution into a series of machine instructions to perform that solution.

compatible: One designation of the computers introduced by most manufacturers in the mid-1960s; these computers are distinguished by their grouping into several families, all of whose members can execute the same programs (within certain limits) without program modification; also featured is a combination of *fixed-word* and *variable-word* operations to accommodate both scientific and business data processing.

compiler: One *software* item which directs computer conversion of a *source program* in other than symbolic form into either symbolic or executable (e.g., *object program*) form; a source program written in COBOL is converted by a COBOL compiler, a FORTRAN source program is converted by a FORTRAN compiler, and so on; *see also* assembly.

computer: Any device able to accept information and modify or manipulate it to produce meaningful results (*see also* digital computer); in this broad sense, an adding machine is a computer.

CPM: Critical path method, one aspect of *PERT*.

data channel width: In *compatible* computer lines, one of the differences among different models in a single line, describing the amount of information exchanged between *main storage* (or *memory*) and the rest of the computer during any one *access* time to storage; all *variable-word* computers have a data channel width of one *character*; *fixed-word* computers have a data channel width of one *word*; *compatible* computer models differ in offering a width of one *byte*, one word (four bytes), or two words (eight bytes).

data processing: A general term for *information* handling, including sorting, classification, recording, calculation, summarization, etc.; commonly restricted to mean either computer or EAM (electric accounting machine) processing of information.

demand processing: Processing of an input or *transaction record* as soon as it becomes available; an airlines reservation system uses demand processing for a minute-by-minute inventory control operation as opposed to an inventory control system that runs only at day's end on the accumulated *batch* to update its master files after all transactions for the day have been completed; sometimes referred to as *real-time, on-line* processing, although real time covers a larger area; also describes multifunction as opposed to dedicated processing systems; for example, a system that processes inventory control, production monitoring, and management information queries intermixed is one form of a demand system, whereas a system that handles only airlines reservations on a "here and now" basis is a dedicated system.

Dennison tickets: See pin-punched tickets.

digital computer: Any device that handles information in the form of discrete numbers (e.g., an adding machine); usually restricted in meaning to high-speed electronic computers which are digital (i.e., count on their fingers) rather than analog (i.e., use a physical quantity like electric current or turns of a wheel to represent other physical quantities).

double word: In a *fixed-word* computer, an information unit twice the length of its *word;* for a *byte*-organized or *compatible* computer, this information unit is 8 bytes (64 *bits*) in length.

dump: A program-testing technique that produces a record of current *memory* contents as an aid in determining what the tested program has done up to the point of the dump.

EBCDIC: Abbreviation for extended *BCD* interchange code; used to describe the 8-bit code (which allows 256 different symbols or *characters* to be represented) used in *compatible* computers.

edit (v): To validate information before it is submitted for processing; to check information submitted to the computer for conformity with prescribed limits (e.g., five-digit account numbers, etc.); to rearrange information within the computer for more comprehensible presentation outside the computer (e.g., introducing spaces between successive fields of a record before printing and suppressing leading [left-hand] zeroes in amount fields).

electromechanical: Using the flow of electricity to control and move mechanical structures such as relays; an electromechanical device is characterized by speeds of hundreds of operations per second in contrast to electronic devices with speeds of millions of operations per second.

electronic: using vacuum tubes, transistors, or other devices that operate by the flow of electrons at ultrahigh speed; contrasted with *electromechanical,* which see.

E-13B: The type name of the characters accepted by the American Bank

Association as standard for their *MICR* encoding on bank checks; the E-13B set includes the digits o through 9, a dash, an amount symbol, a transit (clearing house) symbol, and an "on-us" symbol to set off information of use to the issuing bank (such as the account number and branch).

exception handling: The procedures for dealing with unusual or rare items, to avoid degrading system performance on run-of-the-mill items.

exception reporting: a technique for reducing the volume of output from a processing system by reporting only those results that differ from expectations or rules and require management attention or resolution.

executive: The master program which controls the execution of other programs; sometimes used synonymously with *supervisor.*

field: A subdivision of a *record,* containing one item of information; e.g., an employee's weekly time card contains his identification number in one field; related to *variable-word* in some computers.

fixed point arithmetic: Arithmetic operations that assume the position of the decimal point in each number being processed; for example, fixed point operation with dollars and cents assumes that the decimal point is to the right of the rightmost digit, thus treating the amount as all cents (unless more precision is required, as in interest calculations where tenths or hundredths of a cent may be carried); *see* floating point.

fixed word: A form of computer organization in which its storage contains fixed-sized locations (of *word* size) into which information must be fitted; in general, a computer of this type accesses a full word each time it addresses its storage in contrast to a *variable-word* computer, which accepts only one *character* on each (internal) addressing of storage; a fixed-word organized computer is thus often faster than its opposite number, but may lose this speed advantage if the information does not fit neatly into its word size; *see* compatible.

floating point arithmetic: Arithmetic operations that calculate the position of the decimal point in each result; this form of arithmetic frees the programmer of accounting for the decimal point in his program, but takes more time in execution and can lose some precision in its results; it is used most often in scientific and engineering calculations on limited-precision information and in statistical calculations that are concerned with principal values and not refined results; *see* fixed-point.

flow chart: A graphic presentation of the processing steps in an information processing system which is more or less detailed, depending on the scope covered by the chart.

FORTRAN: Formula translator.

gaming theory: A field of mathematics devoted to simple games of strategy in which the opponent's strategy has an appreciable effect (unlike ticktacktoe, in which a defensive player can always force a draw); sometimes applied to evaluation of sales campaigns in a competitive environment.

half-word: In a *fixed-word* computer, an information unit one-half the length of its *word;* in a *byte*-organized or *compatible* computer, an information unit 2 bytes (16 *bits*) in length.

hardware: The actual equipment making up a computer or EAM system; contrast with *software.*

header card: The first card in a multiple-card record on punched cards; the header card contains the record identification and other information as well; *see* trailer card.

imprinter: A device for adding some printing to an already-printed document; e.g., the gadget that prints from your credit card onto the charge card.

instruction: A direction to the computer to perform one of its basic operations, such as ADD; each instruction calls for the performance of only one operation; *see also* instruction list.

instruction list: The complete repertory of basic operations that the computer can perform, ranging from 40 to over 100 in different computers; each instruction in the list is uniquely identified by its instruction code; a single program will not necessarily use every instruction in the computer list, but it will use those needed to perform the required operations in the appropriate order and as often as needed to accomplish the program objective.

I/O: Abbreviation for input/output, referring to the array of devices through which information is entered into or put out by a computer.

Kimball tickets: See pin-punched tickets.

line printer: An I/O device that produces readable copy at high speeds (e.g., 150 to 1500 lines per minute).

linear programming: A field of mathematics that deals with simple (i.e., linear), sometimes numerous, relations that can be evaluated by a computer; one form of *modeling* or *simulation.*

logic: As used in the computer field, the system that relates the input signals to a computer component with its output; more broadly, within the computer field, the rigorous application of reason to a problem.

magnetic-card array: A *random access* device that features higher capacity than disc or drum, but which has longer access times;

various trade names for this type of device are Data Cell, CRAM, etc.

magnetic disc: A storage device that uses the surfaces of one or more discs for magnetic recording; each surface is divided into *tracks*, which are further divided into *sectors*.

main storage: Computer *memory.*

management by exception: See exception reporting.

management information system: The adaptation or overlay of an information processing system to provide management with the information and control it needs over the area covered by the system; a good computer data processing system includes the elements of a management information system without becoming overbalanced in that direction.

mark sensing: A machine-readable medium that recognizes special pencil marking in particular areas on a form; one example of mark-sense forms is the multitude of machine-markable or gradable multiple-choice test forms.

master file: The collection of records that changes slowly (if at all) with time, and against which *transaction records* are processed; for example, a payroll master file contains a record for each employee, containing his pay rate, Social Security number, number of deductions, withholding obligations (hospitalization insurance, payroll savings, union dues, etc.), address, and so on; the master file may also carry accumulations of previous transactions such as gross earnings to date, amounts withheld for taxes, vacation time accrued, and so on.

memory: Storage section of computer, holding program(s), data, and results.

MICR: Magnetic-ink character recognition, a generic name for machine-readable records that are also human-readable, using magnetizable ink for machine recognition; the most widespread use of MICR in the United States is on bank checks; *see* E-13B.

mnemonic: Literally, easy to remember; more specifically, the abbreviations or code symbols used in symbolic programming languages to designate the various machine instructions; also applied to the symbols or names of locations if these are designed to be understandable as abbreviations.

modeling: The use of a computer to imitate some process or situation represented by a set of mathematical relations that constitute a model of the process or situation; *see* simulation.

monitor: See supervisor.

multiprogramming: The execution of two or more programs within a single, extended time interval, allowing each program to proceed when its requirements (e.g., I/O transfers) are met, but allowing the other program(s) to proceed while the first awaits some requirement.

object program: The result of computer conversion of a *source program;* unless errors have been found, the object program can be executed by the computer.

OCR: Optical character recognition; machine-readable records that depend on character shape rather than magnetic properties of the ink in which they are printed (but *see* MICR); used for gasoline credit cards, on some cash registers, and by the New York State Bureau of Motor Vehicles on registration forms.

off-line: Not directly connected to the computer; in the context of data communications, not directly connected to the transmission line as in keyboarding information onto perforated tape *off-line* for later *on-line* transmission at higher-than-keyboard speed.

on-line: Directly connected to the computer; the significance of this term depends upon your point of view, whether from inside or outside the computer; for example, a line printer can be fed directly from the computer, putting it on-line to the computer, or the computer can put out its records for printing onto magnetic tape (which is then read through another computer to its printer), putting the printer *off-line* to the first computer; conversely, an airlines reservations clerk is on-line to his computer because he enters a request for information that is answered directly by the computer; the clerk's impression is quite correct from his point of view even though his request is accumulated outside the computer before it is entered, and the computer services that request when it gets to it; this occurs many operations later, by computer time, but almost instantaneously in the clerk's reference frame.

operand: The item operated on by an instruction; the operands of an ADD instruction are the two numbers to be added.

operating system: A utility program system that schedules the operation of a computer in executing *batch processing* for maximum computer utilization; similar to a *supervisor,* although the operating system may not handle all input/output operations for application programs.

operations research: A field of applied mathematics devoted to the development of mathematical models of real situations or processes, said models being manipulatable by computer to reveal the relations among the controlled and uncontrolled variables in the model; the model may be simplified with respect to the real world, for ease in manipulation; its validity must always temper the acceptance of conclusions drawn from its performance.

packed format: Decimal numbers in *BCD* (or *EBCDIC*) which have had their *zone bits* removed from all but one digit; a packed decimal number takes less storage space than an *unpacked* decimal number, four bits per digit as compared with six (or eight in EBCDIC); also the storage of two (or more) information items in one *word.*

paper tape: One form of *perforated tape;* other forms use metal foil, polyester bases (e.g., Mylar), and sandwiches of these materials.

perforated tape: A recording medium like punched cards, but not restricted to 80-character records; often produced as a by-product of keyboarding on a properly equipped typewriter or a teletype unit.

PERT: Program evaluation and review technique.

pin-punched tickets: Small tags with small holes that code the merchandise characteristics; used for inventory control or sales analysis of clothing items by department stores; often described as *Kimball* or *Dennison* tags, after two competing suppliers.

problem definition: The first phase of computer programming, reducing the problem to a form that allows machine solution; *see* systems analysis, coding.

problem-oriented language: A computer programming language that uses the terminology "natural" to the problem area rather than to the computer to be used; such languages are usually also machine-independent; examples include COBOL, PL/I, etc.

procedure-oriented language: Similar to *problem-oriented language* but often more general in application; for example, FORTRAN is a procedure-oriented language, accommodating common mathematical expressions with little or no change.

process control: The application of a computer to a continuously changing situation (e.g., oil refinery, power distribution network, etc.) to control and maintain optimum performance of the controlled system; a truly *real-time* system that demands most of the computer capabilities just to keep up with the controlled system.

program (n): The sequence of *instructions* that directs a computer in its performance in solving a problem.

program (v). To prepare the sequence of instructions for a computer; usually divided into two phases, the first being problem definition (or *systems analysis*) and the second being *coding.*

punched card: A machine-readable medium commonly used in EAM and in computer systems; each punched card can hold 80 (or 90 in some designs) characters in *BCD* code; the punched card is one of the cheapest mediums of storage and one of the most widely used.

query-response system: One form of *demand processing* in which the user operates in *real* (to him) *time* with the computer; this form of processing gives each user the sense of being master of the computer, whereas it is actually serving all masters and, possibly, doing a good bit of *batch processing* on the side (in the *background*); some *process control* systems (notably those for air traffic or air defense) include a query-response subsystem to service their human masters while they spend the bulk of their (high-speed) time maintaining the picture of things as they were an instant ago, said picture being the source of answers to the human queries; not all query-response systems include a process control system (e.g., airlines reservations) unless the source of answers changes at a high (to the computer) rate.

random access: A storage medium characteristic, indicating that records are available (more or less) independently of their location in the storage medium; computer *main storage* (magnetic cores) is fully random access, whereas other storage media only approximate this randomness or independence of location; contrasted to *sequential access;* examples of random access media include magnetic drums, magnetic discs, magnetic-card arrays, etc.

real time: Most generally, "here and now" time, by the clock rather than by some arbitrary time scale; a system that only keeps up with its human user is often called a "real-time system," whereas the term is better applied to a system that devotes most of its activities to keeping current with a constantly changing situation; *see* process control.

record: A group of related information items treated as a logical unit; usually, a record is divided into one or more *fields*, each containing a different subitem of information.

relative address: The designation of a storage location, in symbolic programming, by indicating how far it is from another location; i.e., relative to that other location.

run (n): A complete sequence of processing by a computer on one submission of input data, requiring little or no operator action after he sets it up; usually limited in its processing capability by the number of I/O devices on the computer and by the computer storage size.

run (v): To execute a program or a complete subportion of a program on a computer.

sector: A portion of a *track* on a *magnetic disc* surface, usually a separately addressable portion.

sequential access: A storage medium characteristic, indicating that records are available sequentially (one after the other) in some fixed order; contrasted to *random access;* examples of sequential access media include punched cards, perforated tape, magnetic tape, etc.

significance coding: Assignment of identification codes with inherent meaning to items identified; for example, Selective Service numbers identify the draft board, the date of issue, and the individual in question; contrasted with arbitrary coding in which the identification codes have no meaning.

simulation: A technique of computer usage that employs the computer as an imitator or modeler of some other situation or process to obtain, inexpensively, some indication of results from the simulated situation or process.

software: The set of programs used with a computer to write other programs, perform standard operations, or to make the computer appear to be another machine; often extended to include the applications programs (problem solving) run on the *hardware* and *software* combination.

sorting: The process of placing items in order on some key (e.g., account number or inventory description number).

source program: A program written in symbolic or other nonexecutable form (e.g., COBOL, FORTRAN) and submitted for computer conversion into executable form: *see* object program.

storage: Any medium in which information can be held; written documents, recordings of dictation, punched cards, magnetic tape, etc., all constitute forms of storage; in connection with a computer, *storage* normally refers to the computer main *memory*, usually magnetic cores.

storage cycle: The time taken to read a main storage location in the computer and to write its contents back into the same location; also the time between successive accesses to the same storage array; sometimes referred to as the computer's *unit-time interval;* this time is generally longer than the *access time* for the main storage.

stored program: Characteristic of a computer that retains its *program* internally, allowing it to modify its program in response to the results of its calculations; contrasted with fixed or externally programmed devices, neither of which allows program modification in the same way.

subsystem: An isolable portion of a system; a subsystem is treated as a complete system while its interactions with other elements of the larger system to which it belongs are ignored.

supervisor: A program that controls computer input/output operations and acts as traffic clerk for all computer operations, including scheduling of application program execution; most *compatible* computers require a supervisor program for efficient use of the computer; *see also* operating system.

symbolic address: The address of a storage location designated by an arbitrary name or label rather than as an *absolute address.*

symbolic programming: A machine-oriented programming system that relegates to the computer much of the bookkeeping involved in producing an executable program; this form of *coding* uses *mnemonics* to designate machine instructions, *symbols* or labels to name or identify storage locations, and *relative addresses* rather than *absolute addresses;* a symbolic program must be translated with an *assembly* program by the computer before it can be executed.

system: An organized whole; the complete assemblage of personnel, equipment, and procedures which accomplishes an overall purpose; the organization of a system may be inherent in it or imposed from outside.

systems analysis: The examination of a procedure or a segment of business operation to determine its requirements and the best means of accomplishing them; usually, but not necessarily, the examination considers the best means for computer accomplishment.

time broker: A dealer in computer time, selling at retail to prospective users or simply matching prospective users with potential time sellers in return for a commission.

time sharing: Generally, the use of a computer for more than one application at a time by allocating successive time slots to active applications; a more restrictive sense of this phrase describes multiple-user access to a computer in "real-to-each-user time"; in this sense, an airlines reservation system is a time-sharing system.

total system: A philosophy of computer application that integrates all information processing within an area (or a company) for processing by the computer, minimizing clerical operations and human activities in the area.

trace: A program-testing technique that records selected storage locations before and after execution of the program instructions being traced, producing a dynamic record of that portion of program results.

track: The area swept on a magnetic recording device by a read-write head.

trailer card: The second and succeeding card(s) in a multiple-card record on punched cards; each trailer card carries some identification to associate it with its record and to indicate its position in the sequence of cards carrying that record; also, the trailer card carries additional information for that record; *see* header card.

transaction record: A record of data to be entered against a *master file* record; a weekly time card, a charge-out from inventory, a record of receipt of ordered goods, a request for a seat on a given airline flight—all are transaction records.

transfer rate: The rate in characters or bytes per second at which information can be moved into or out of a storage medium; the transfer rate for computer main storage is the reciprocal of its storage cycle and is thus related to its *access time;* for other *random access* storage devices, the transfer rate is not related to the access time.

turnaround technique: The use of a computer-originated document as input to a later computer run; e.g., the payment stub on a credit card or utilities bill.

turnaround time: The elapsed time between submission of data and program to a computer and the return of processed data; this time can run from 24 to 48 hours in a large *batch processing* system.

unit-time interval: The minimum time between successive accesses to computer main storage, either to obtain an *instruction* or an *operand* (i.e., an information unit to be processed).

unpacked format: Decimal numbers in *BCD* (or *EBCDIC*) with their *zone bits* present; i.e., all six (or eight) bits per digit.

utilization factor: The ratio of computer time used to computer time available; a measure of machine employment but not of system efficiency.

variable word: A form of computer organization in which its storage contains locations of *character* size which can be designated as part of a variable-size *word* or *field;* no storage space is wasted on undersized information units (undersized in comparison to a fixed word, that is), but the computer accesses only one character at a time from storage, using several storage cycles to process a single word even though the programmer *addresses* the word, not its individual characters; *see* fixed word.

verification: A checking operation following the punching of punched cards to determine that the correct information has been punched; the verification operator keys in the same information that was used to punch the cards, and this is compared with what is punched in the cards, to determine any differences or possible errors.

word: A larger information unit than the *character* (6 bits) or *byte* (8 bits); formed on the analogy that several characters in English make up a word; sometimes used interchangeably with *field;* in *byte*-organized computers, a *word* contains 4 bytes (32 bits).

zone bits: The added bits (two or four) that add the capability of representing letters to the decimal-digit representation possible with four-bit *BCD* codes; sometimes used to represent the sign (+ or −) of a decimal number in *BCD*.

BIBLIOGRAPHY

BOOKS

CANNING, RICHARD G. *Electronic Data Processing for Business and Industry.* New York: John Wiley & Sons, 1956. An excellent, if dated, presentation of the subject, still worth reading for its understandability despite concentration on now-superceded approaches (e.g., file processors).

HALACY, D. S., JR. *Computers: The Machines We Think With.* New York: Harper & Row, 1962. Layman's introduction to the computer, covers in detail the fundamentals of computer technology.

LAZZARO, VICTOR (ed.). *Systems and Procedures; A Handbook for Business and Industry.* New York: Prentice-Hall, 1958. A workbook treatment in detail of system design, independent of computers.

NEUSCHEL, RICHARD F. *Management by System.* New York: McGraw-Hill, 1960. A well-written guide to management for redesigning its information processing.

RADAMAKER, TED (ed.). *Business Systems* (2 vols.). Cleveland: Systems & Procedures Association, 1963. Aimed at the office or plant manager who wishes to redesign his information processing system; covers the area in considerable detail.

SIMON, HERBERT A. *The New Science of Management Decision.* New York: Harper & Row, 1960. A forward-looking treatment of the scientific methods, implemented by computer processing, for improved management decision-making.

PERIODICALS

The following magazines are all available by subscription; some, however, are also available on a controlled circulation basis to qualified subscribers without fee. In either case, the publisher is usually willing to supply a sample copy without charge.

Automation, The Penton Publishing Company, Penton Building, Cleveland 13, Ohio. Intended for the business user of punched-card accounting and small computer systems; applications oriented.

Business Automation, OA Business Publications, 600 W. Jackson Blvd., Chicago, Ill. (controlled circulation). Intended for the neophyte in business applications of computer and machine accounting systems; also covers a broad range of non-data processing office equipment.

Computers and Automation, Berkeley Enterprises Inc., 815 Washington St., Newtonville, Mass. 02160. Aimed at the data processing manager rather than noncomputer management but surveys new developments in the field, both technical and marketing.

Computers and Data Processing, Nielson Publishing Company, 217 Broadway, New York, N.Y. 10007 (controlled circulation). Like *Computers and Automation* but, so far, less given to survey or "directory" issues which enhance the value of its competitor.

Data Processing Magazine, 134 N. 13th St., Philadelphia, Pa. 19107. Stresses sub-computer systems but is less applications oriented than *Automation.*

Datamation, F. D. Thompson Publications, 141 E. 44th St., New York, N.Y. 10017 (controlled circulation). Aimed at the managerial and technical people in the data processing field, stressing new developments in system programs, hardware, applications, etc. Shows a sense of humor and is the standard against which its competitors are measured.

Journal of Machine Accounting, Data Processing Management Association, 524 Busse Highway, Park Ridge, Ill. 60068. Initially heavy on EAM (punched card) procedures, tending more now into the small computer field; intended for technical personnel in the field.

Modern Office Procedures, 812 Huron Road, Cleveland 15, Ohio (controlled circulation). Wide-ranging coverage of office equipment, from electric wastebaskets (shredders) through microfilm and small computer systems.

Systems and Procedures Journal, Systems & Procedures Association, Penobscot Building, Detroit, Mich. Intended for systems people in the EAM and computer fields; comparable to *Journal of Machine Accounting* but with stronger system orientation.

The Office, Office Publications Co., 232 Madison Ave., New York, N.Y. 10016. Comparable to *Modern Office Procedures.*

OTHER PUBLICATIONS

The computer manufacturers (e.g., IBM, UNIVAC, RCA, Honeywell, GE, etc.) offer many worthwhile publications on the subjects of computers and computer applications. These documents are obtainable through each manufacturer's local sales representative.

The American Management Association, 135 W. 50th St., New York, N.Y. 10021, produces a series of publications intended for management, some of which pertain to management uses of the computer. These publications are available on loan to AMA members or can be purchased. Consult the AMA directly for its current catalog.

Several companies which supply materials used by computers offer application notes on solutions to users' problems. Notable among these suppliers are Moore Business Forms, Inc., Niagara Falls, N.Y., and The Standard Register Company, Dayton, Ohio 45401.

INDEX

Absolute machine language, 53, 55, 58, 59, 162
Access, sequential and random, 16-21; *see also* Random access; Sequential access
Access, time, 21, 23, 28, 30, 33, 34, 198
Accounting, 67, 148, 171; fraud with computers, 141, 144-146; general ledger, 3, 9; taxation and, 191
Accounts payable, 3, 119, 144
Accounts receivable, 3, 5, 144
ADD (mnemonic code), 55, 203, 205
Add-on memory units, 21-22
Address, 10, 30, 159, 198; machine language and, 53, 55, 56; relative, 207; symbolic, 208
Administration. *See* Management
Aerospace industy, 4, 188
Air conditioning, 168-169
Airlines: reservations system, 18, 19, 120, 200-201; traffic control, 20
American Banking Association, 24, 201
American Standards Code for Information Interchange (ASCII), 23, 198
American Telephone and Telegraph Company, 23 *n.*, 42 *n.*
Analog computers, 7, 20, 201
Aptitude tests, 156
Arithmetic. *See* Binary arithmetic; Mathematical uses
Arithmetic and logic unit, 8

ASCII (American Standards Code for Information Interchange), 23, 198
Assembler program, 55-56, 128, 162, 198

Banking, 18, 24-25, 30, 68; computer contracts and, 142; computer rental services in, 119, 120; loan terms, 193; query-response system, 37; wage levels in, 156
Batch processing, 19, 21, 37, 96, 199; capacity reservation and, 127; classification coding in, 110; centralized data conversion and, 114; corrections and, 161; display devices, 36; input data collection for, 17, 18, 20, 39-45; payroll, 47-49; personnel in, 62, 64, 157; system design and, 113, 121, 124-125; tape drives and, 30, 124; volume and, 81-83, 118
BCD. *See* Binary-coded decimal numbers (BCD)
Bell Telephone System, 42, 99
Benchmark problem, 128, 130, 132, 134, 136
Billing services, 119
Binary arithmetic, 12-13, 14, 60-61
Binary-coded decimal (BCD), 12-13, 14, 199, 201, 205
Binary digit (bit), 11, 12, 13, 199
Business machine composite systems: equipment manufacturers, 123; feasibility, 96, 97, 98-99, 100-